Economics Is Everywhere

Economics Is Everywhere

DANIEL S. HAMERMESH

University of Texas at Austin

Boston   Burr Ridge, IL   Dubuque, IA   Madison, WI   New York
San Francisco   St. Louis   Bangkok   Bogotá   Caracas   Kuala Lumpur
Lisbon   London   Madrid   Mexico City   Milan   Montreal   New Delhi
Santiago   Seoul   Singapore   Sydney   Taipei   Toronto

Irwin

ECONOMICS IS EVERYWHERE
Published by McGraw-Hill/Irwin, a business unit of The McGraw-Hill
Companies, Inc., 1221 Avenue of the Americas, New York, NY, 10020. Copyright
© 2004 by The McGraw-Hill Companies, Inc. All rights reserved. No part of this
publication may be reproduced or distributed in any form or by any means, or
stored in a database or retrieval system, without the prior written consent of
The McGraw-Hill Companies, Inc., including, but not limited to, in any network
or other electronic storage or transmission, or broadcast for distance learning.
Some ancillaries, including electronic and print components, may not be
available to customers outside the United States.

This book is printed on acid-free paper.

3 4 5 6 7 8 9 0 DOC/DOC 0 9 8 7 6 5 4 3

ISBN 0-07-285143-0

Publisher: *Gary Burke*
Executive sponsoring editor: *Paul Shensa*
Editorial assistant: *Jennifer Leon*
Marketing manager: *Martin D. Quinn*
Lead project manager: *Mary Conzachi*
Senior production supervisor: *Michael R. McCormick*
Lead designer: *Pam Verros*
Typeface: *10.5/12 Palatino*
Compositor: *Lachina Publishing Services*
Printer: *R. R. Donnelley*
Cover art: *Photographer: ©The Solomon R. Guggenheim Foundation, New York
Vasily Kandinsky* Upward, *October 1929/Oil on cardboard 27^1/$_2$ × 19^1/$_4$ (70 × 49
cms). The Solomon R. Guggenheim Foundation, New York, Peggy Guggenheim
Collection, Venice, 1976. 76.2553.35*

Library of Congress Cataloging-in-Publication Data

Hamermesh, Daniel S.
    Economics is everywhere / Daniel S. Hamermesh.
        p. cm.
    Includes index.
    ISBN 0-07-285143-0 (alk. paper)
    1. Microeconomics. 2. Economics. I. Title.
HB172 .H364 2004
338.5--dc21
                                                            2002514119

www.mhhe.com

Preface

For over thirty years I have been bringing unusual stories into my micro principles classes and commenting on them from an economic viewpoint. At the start of the fall semester of 2001 I began doing this in the usual way. One student pointed out that it would help her if I would post these stories and my comments on them on my website; that way she could look at them later and use them to help her study for exams. I began posting these comments on a regular basis, creating an entry in what I called the "Economic Thought of the Day." A few of my friends and colleagues saw these postings and pointed out that with some expansion they would make a nice supplement to a micro principles course. This is the result.

The vignettes are organized in the same order as the topics that make up my introductory microeconomics course. This arrangement corresponds quite closely to the plans of most micro principles texts. A few texts, however, include international trade (particularly comparative advantage) as the second topic in the course, immediately after supply and demand. For teachers using such books Chapter 21 can be assigned right after Chapter 1 or, better still, after Chapter 7.

I thank James Barbour, Valerie Bencivenga, Anne Golla, Stephen Lich-Tyler, Paul Shensa, and Max Stinchcombe for their extremely helpful suggestions and comments on the manuscript, and Lawrence Hamermesh and John Siegfried for their encouragement. A number of colleagues, students, and family members made suggestions that led to the vignettes included here, and others' behavior inspired some vignettes. This volume is dedicated to Frances W. Hamermesh, who commented on the entire manuscript, inspired many of the examples, and has encouraged and supported this project and everything else in my professional and personal lives for thirty-seven years.

Daniel S. Hamermesh
Austin
June 2002

About the Author

Daniel S. Hamermesh is the Edward Everett Hale Centennial Professor of Economics at the University of Texas at Austin. He received his B.A. from the University of Chicago (1965) and his Ph.D. from Yale University (1969). He taught from 1969–73 at Princeton, from 1973–93 at Michigan State, and has held visiting professorships at universities in the United States, Europe, Australia, and Asia. He is a Fellow of the Econometric Society, a Research Associate of the National Bureau of Economic Research, Program Director at the Forschungsinstitut zur Zukunft der Arbeit (IZA), and past president of the Society of Labor Economists and of the Midwest Economics Association. He authored *Labor Demand* and *The Economics of Work and Pay*, and a wide array of articles in labor economics in the leading general and specialized economics journals. His research concentrates on labor demand, time use, and unusual applications of labor economics (to suicide, sleep, and beauty). He has taught introductory microeconomics since 1968 to over 10,000 students.

Contents

Thinking about Economics Everywhere

In every introductory microeconomics course you are taught a large number of technical, jargon-type words. These words represent a form of shorthand, a way to summarize ideas about behavior. There is one word that I teach the very first day of my introductory class, and I believe it is the most important of all: *empathy*—the intellectual identification with the feelings, thoughts, or attitudes of someone else. A student should put himself or herself into the particular problem being discussed and ask, "How would I behave if I were confronted with those choices?" Microeconomics is very logical, and most of us think very logically in our daily lives. When confronted with economic questions, though, we too often forget our logic and get scared because somehow the questions seem different. They're not: The economic issues pose the same questions that are posed to us in many of our daily activities and that we almost always answer sensibly and correctly.

The purpose of this book is to illustrate the wide range of daily activities to which an economic way of thinking can be applied. Some of the 400 vignettes are dated to indicate that they were inspired by something that came up on that particular day, but most arose from more general musing. They are organized according to the topical arrangement of a typical introductory microeconomics course. That way they can tie into what you are learning from any standard introductory textbook. They can focus your ability to apply the formal analysis taught in class to the myriad examples that come out of our daily activities. After studying this book you should be able to see your own activities and the things that you read in newspapers, magazines, and books or hear on television in a new, economic way. As a result you should be able to understand your world better.

Ideally you should read and think about the material in this book in small bits at a time—not all at once and not even each chapter at once. Reading and thinking about a few vignettes a day is the best way to learn from this material how to think in economic terms about everyday phenomena. A vignette in Chapter 9 gives good economic reasons why you may not want to do this, but it is the best way to learn from this volume. After reading a vignette you should go directly to the attached question and try answering it while the thought expressed in the vignette is fresh in your mind.

PART I

*T*rade-Offs, Supply, and Demand

CHAPTER 1

*T*rade-Offs and Opportunity Cost

1.1

Mick Jagger sang, "You can't always get what you want." This is the essence of economics: Wants are unlimited, but the resources to satisfy them are *scarce*. That's true for us as individuals, and it's also true for societies. In the same song he also states, "And if you try sometime you find you get what you need." This statement makes no economic sense. *Needs* is not an economic term. I "need" tickets to the ballet once a week, my private jet with pilot, my home theater, and a chauffeur for the limousine I would like to own. Nobody has the right to argue with my statement about what I "need." Unfortunately, I do not have the income to obtain all these things; and even if I did, the scarcity imposed by the twenty-four-hour day would prevent me from enjoying them in the style I would like. I can satisfy my basic wants; I can afford the time and income for the things that are most important to me. But we all define our needs so broadly that Mick is wrong—you can never get what you need!

> *Q: Make a list of ten things that you "need." Do you get them all? If not, is it because your income isn't high enough or because you haven't got enough time?*

1.2

In the movie *The Hand That Rocks the Cradle*, a female character makes the comment, "Today's woman has to do three things: bring

home at least $50,000 per year, [. . .], and cook homemade lasagna."
It is unlikely that many women will be able to do all three,
because the first and third are probably **substitutes**. A woman
who is earning that much money is unlikely to have the time to
cook homemade lasagna because there is a **scarcity** of time, her
most important resource. The opposite side of the coin is that a
woman who has chosen to spend time rolling homemade pasta
is unlikely to have enough time to earn this much. ([. . .] probably
can be done by both high-earning women and those who have
chosen to stay at home.) But fixed resources—twenty-four hours
in the day—make it unlikely that most women will be able to do
all three things.

> *Q: Are the **opportunity costs** of earning and cooking constant
> over the day and the week, or can women (and men too) find times
> when one is relatively cheap and the other is relatively costly?
> What are these times?*

1.3

One of my female colleagues commented on the previous entry,
stating, "I earn more than $50,000, and I also make homemade
lasagna." My response was that **production possibility frontiers**
differ, depending on a person's or country's resources and technology. She is very efficient at many things and can both earn a
lot and make great home-cooked lasagna. Nonetheless, even she
faces a **trade-off**, assuming that she is working and enjoying
leisure efficiently. If she works more, she can earn more, but she
will have less time for home cooking. If she cooks more, she
won't be able to earn so much.

> *Q: Draw her **production possibility frontier** in these two
> activities. Now draw a point that accounts for the fact that she
> spends one hour a day doing absolutely nothing.*

1.4

September 13, 2001—My wife and I donate over $100 for relief
for the September 11, 2001, New York terrorist attack. But our
five-year-old grandson has offered to give $1 of his savings to
help out. We have a much higher income than our grandson; in

fact, he doesn't earn a penny, relying only on a tiny allowance from his parents. Who is sacrificing more—whose **opportunity cost** of the contribution is greater—our grandson's or ours?

> *Q: Does the fact that our grandson and we are responding to the need for contributions after September 11 make our **opportunity cost** any different from what it would be if the charitable request were, for example, for the local United Way?*

1.5

October 1, 2001—Forcing us to spend more resources on security (using the National Guard at airports, more checkpoints entering the United States, etc.) is in the end the biggest triumph by terrorists. The government pays National Guard troops, and since the guardspeople are not at their regular jobs, output outside the security sector is diminished. The output of the security people doesn't give us anything that we would want if there were no perceived need for security. The resources used for this purpose are like a negative change in technology; they shift the **production possibility frontier** inward. In this case, unlike in the example of Mick Jagger's singing, our behavior implies that our desire for security is a basic need—it comes before anything else.

> *Q: Is this vignette correct? After all, the security guards get paid and buy things, so aren't they adding to output?*

1.6

A great example of **trade-offs** comes from the life of a full-time student. Such students can be imagined as having only two uses of their time—studying and socializing—and two outputs from those uses—knowledge acquired and social satisfaction. If a student is efficient, he or she cannot increase the amount of knowledge acquired in college without giving up social satisfaction. The **opportunity cost** of one more unit of social satisfaction is some amount of forgone knowledge, and the opportunity cost of another unit of knowledge is forgone social satisfaction. This **production possibility frontier** can shift out along each axis. A speed-reading course moves the curve out along the axis for knowledge acquisition, allowing the student to obtain *both* more knowledge and more social satisfaction (because some time that can be saved from studying can be shifted to socializing). It's harder to think of improvements that move the curve out along the social satisfaction axis. One regrettably out-of-date example is the "Orgasmatron" in Woody Allen's movie *Sleeper*.

> *Q: Draw the production possibility frontier implied in this vignette. List one other example of a technical improvement that shifts the frontier out the learning axis, one other that shifts it out the social satisfaction axis, and one that simultaneously shifts it out both axes.*

1.7

While stranded on an airplane at the Dallas–Fort Worth airport, I was able to call the reservation number from my cell phone and rebook myself onto a later plane (since I was going to miss my connection). Without the cell phone I would have had to line up at the pay phone after getting off the plane. Technological improvements save us time or allow things to be produced more cheaply, but they also enable us to do things that make us better off that we would never have thought of doing.

> *Q: You have drawn **production possibility frontiers** in class. How would you draw what happens to the production possibility frontier in the case outlined in this vignette?*

1.8

The main function of the College of Liberal Arts Promotion and Tenure Committee is to discuss granting lifetime tenure to faculty members at the end of their probationary periods (typically six years). The dean of the college, a professor of Sanskrit, asked the following question: "Could we do better hiring a person from outside the university in place of the person we are considering for promotion? After all, we are granting someone a salary of at least $60,000 a year for the remainder of his or her career." The **opportunity cost** of granting a lifetime job to a professor is the benefits that could be obtained from an alternative use of the salary the professor would be paid over his or her lifetime.

Q: Let's say the typical professor earns $60,000 per year. What is the opportunity cost of granting lifetime tenure to a thirty-five-year-old professor who will work until age seventy?

1.9

A constant complaint by longer-term residents (more than one year) in rapidly growing Austin, Texas, is that the city is "too crowded." People complain about the traffic, crowded parks and swimming holes, and so on. They never complain about the growth in the number and variety of restaurants, theaters, and cultural events or about the increase in specialized retail outlets in town. The two are related: Bigger cities bring broader and more diverse culture and activities. The **trade-off** is that they also bring more crowds and traffic congestion. New people, those who made the choice to accept the crowds in exchange for more excitement, are clearly better off. Longer-term residents may indeed be worse off because they chose to come to the area when the trade-off was different. Some of them may have benefited from the trade-off: They may like the greater breadth of activities more than they dislike the added congestion. Other longer-term residents, though, may be worse off: The change in the trade-off goes against the preferences that initially drew them to Austin.

*Q: Graph the **production possibility frontier** implied by this discussion, labeling the axes carefully. [Hint: One "good" might be speed and ease of access to stores, theaters, malls, and so on.] How would that frontier shift if a new invention allowed everyone to move around town twice as fast?*

1.10

Most of the techno-toys we buy—computers, PDAs, and the like—make us better off (otherwise we wouldn't buy them). Most also involve a **trade-off** between cost and convenience: They save time and improve our lives, but they cost more to buy than the items they replaced. Very few such toys both make us better off *and* reduce our total dollar expenditure. This was true even for such techno-toys of the 1940s and 1950s as automatic washers and dryers and TVs. One is my cell phone. Because night and weekend minutes are essentially free, now that we're using the cell phone for long-distance calls, our regular phone bill has fallen by more than the monthly cost of the cell phone plan.

> *Q: Name technical improvements in your life that have actually reduced the dollars you spend on the general activities that the improvements are part of.*

1.11

Many students believe that professors are either good researchers or good teachers but not both. This belief implies that there is a negative relationship between research and teaching comparing across different professors. I don't believe this is true at all: The better researchers are also the better teachers. This doesn't mean that professors have no **trade-offs** in their activities. Instead, those who are good at one thing are good at the other, and those who are mediocre at one are typically mediocre at both. There is a trade-off for each individual, but the overall level of ability differs among professors so that some professors can perform better in both areas.

> *Q: Draw the production possibility curves for a high-ability professor and a low-ability professor that are implied by this vignette. Label the axes carefully.*

1.12

A student told me that she bought a "Hook 'em Horns" souvenir cap through eBay (for her boyfriend, who goes to Texas A&M). She paid $10. Why are people spending time selling very low-value items on eBay? Surely the amount they earn from these sales cannot justify the time spent setting up the auction; the hourly wage they make has got to be below any reasonable estimate of the **opportunity cost** of their time. A lot of the eBay material is sold there because of the novelty of running one's own auction and the fun of playing on the Web this way. eBay auctions are at least in part consumption for both sellers and buyers.

> *Q: Perhaps the vignette misses the point by focusing on **trade-offs** at a single point in time. Might spending your time using*

eBay now be a method of learning that allows you to be much more efficient when you want to auction other, more valuable items in the future?

1.13

January 2, 2002—The most important economic event yesterday was the switchover from the twelve old European currencies to the euro. Like every potentially long-term beneficial change, it may come with short-run costs. Perhaps the most bizarre such reported cost was mentioned in a Reuters story: "One Italian survey found that the stress of it all is affecting the health of bank and shop workers, with symptoms including headaches, insomnia, and even loss of sex drive." One must assume that these transition problems, if they are real, are short-term indeed and that the long-run benefits of the euro—avoiding the costs of converting currencies, enabling consumers and firms to compare prices internationally more easily—shift the **production possibility frontier** out far enough to outweigh even the loss of sex drive among Italians.

> *Q: This vignette talks about a technical improvement that shifts a production possibility frontier outward. We draw those frontiers on a graph with two goods, one on each axis of the graph. What goods would you label the axes with?*

1.14

A student e-mailed an interesting question: "You spent all the time in class talking about technical progress and how it shifts the **production possibility frontier** outward. Has there ever been a case of technical regression that shifted it inward?" If there were a nuclear disaster and we actually lost technology (forgot how to manufacture chips, lost the art of internal combustion, etc.), it would make sense to characterize this as a reduction in technology. (Of course, if we fell back that far, there probably wouldn't be people teaching the idea of production possibility frontiers in colleges.) The only real-life example might be the loss of certain technologies that the Romans developed—internal plumbing and a few others—that were not rediscovered until after the 1600s at least. That would be the best, although very outdated, example of a technological regression.

Q: Technical regression for a society is extremely rare. Cases where a household sees an inward shift in what it can produce are more common. List some things that might cause such an inward shift to occur for a single household.

1.15

Next Saturday is my aged parents' wedding anniversary. I have been wracking my brain, but after all these years it is impossible to think of a present to send them. It suddenly hit me that a good present would be one that costs no money (I'll be using airplane mileage to get a "free ticket") but has an extremely high **opportunity cost**: I'll visit them for a day, fly from Texas to Minnesota next Saturday, and come home next Sunday. I told my mom about this, and she was delighted. Listening to her, I believe that she understands that the opportunity cost to me is high, and that seems to make her appreciate the visit even more. But is the airplane ticket really free? While I pay out no money, the mileage I use for this ticket could be used at a future date for another air ticket. Even if no dollars are spent, and even if no time is consumed, the opportunity cost of the "free ticket" can still be positive.

Q: List two cases where you have spent no money but there were opportunity costs of your time and of something else that could have been bought at a future date.

1.16

At a professional conference in Milan, Italy, several years ago I received a CD of old operatic recordings from La Scala (Milan's famed opera house). I was listening to them again and marveling at the enhancement of well-being produced by technology. Here I was in Texas, listening to long-dead singers doing something beautifully, better than almost anyone does today. Moreover, to me the **opportunity cost** of listening is just my time—no admission ticket, no travel cost, nothing. CDs and their predecessors, tapes and records, are some of the best examples of **technological improvements** that enhance our satisfaction. Nothing like them existed before the twentieth century, and most of us would agree that they have expanded the range of choices of consumption that are open to us.

> *Q: Give two examples of technological innovations that are at least as different as CDs are from anything that came before them.*

1.17

February 9, 2002—Coming home from Minneapolis last Sunday I was one of two unlucky people pulled out of the line at the gate and subjected to a very detailed search. Only one other person, a petite young woman, was searched the same way. I had a free ticket obtained with frequent-flyer mileage; as a fifty-eight-year-old male I doubt that I fit the terrorist profile. Yet substantial resources were spent ensuring that I was not carrying shoe bombs or any other bombs or weapons onto the airplane. Resources for screening are limited, so why should they be wasted in detailed searches of people like me? I suppose the answer is that airline security might otherwise be accused of racial profiling. The airlines—and society—face a **trade-off**: appear fair and spend scarce resources searching low-risk people or single out those who may fit the profile, have a better chance of catching would-be hijackers, but apply the searches in a way that may be perceived as ethnically biased.

> *Q: My time and that of the screeners is easily valued and represents a clear loss of resources to society. Can you compare that measurable loss to the unmeasurable loss that may result from creating the perception of ethnic or racial profiling?*

1.18

March 12, 2002—With the six-month anniversary of the September 11 terror has come a substantial debate over the use of the land where the World Trade Center stood. Survivors want the whole area turned into a memorial. The economic issue is: How much does society want to spend on this memorial? The cost of devoting all sixteen acres to the memorial is the **opportunity cost** of the land: the value in its best nonmemorial use (for commercial real estate). Making the whole area into a memorial is really an economic choice: How much does society want to spend in terms of valuable land left unproductive? The decision is a political one, but it should be informed by comparing the economic costs to the benefits.

Q: How would you calculate the opportunity cost of the sixteen-acre site?

1.19

Opportunity Cost and the "Terrible Twos." Our two-year-old granddaughter typically gets read to and put to bed by her mom, while her dad reads to and puts her older brother to bed. Last night the parents switched, and the little girl cried until her mom reverted to her usual role. Tonight her mom was away for the evening, and so her dad read to her. She sniffled a bit initially, then looked around and realized there was no alternative—her mom wasn't there. She calmed down, understanding even at age two that when the **opportunity cost** is very high, one needs to be satisfied with an otherwise less desirable **substitute**.

Q: Can you put a dollar figure on the opportunity cost here? If not, does that mean that the concept is useless in this case? Give two other examples where you can't measure opportunity cost but believe the concept is relevant.

1.20

On the *Tonight Show* Jay Leno commented that some Hollywood stars are paying people $5,000 per week to keep them off drugs. He noted that they could instead buy the crack cocaine they would like for only $3,500 per week. Here's a rare example of a negative **opportunity cost**: For these people it's cheaper to use crack than not to use it. Buying the crack, if they must otherwise use the services of the drug-prevention specialist, saves them $1,500 per week. If crack cocaine weren't illegal and assuming they enjoy it and suffer no physical damage that limits their future enjoyment and earning power, all the stars would be using it. It is illegal, though, and using crack and getting caught lands them in jail and hurts their careers. In the long run, the opportunity cost of the crack is quite high, as it must include the earnings they will have to forgo if crack usage hurts their careers.

Q: How would the opportunity cost of staying off drugs change if drug usage were legalized? Would the change be more or less for a Hollywood star or for an economics professor?

1.21

The editor's comment in *Celebrated Living*, American Airlines' quarterly luxury magazine, is, "[Our] covers have featured some of the world's most high-profile celebrities, including Michael Jordan, Robert Redford, Clint Eastwood, Giorgio Armani, and Claudia Schiffer. In each interview, these fascinating people all singled out the same thing as the ultimate luxury: time." That is no doubt true for them: They all have enough income to buy all the goods and services they could want. Their "problem" is that like you and me, they have only twenty-four hours a day to consume those goods. They can hire people to do things for them, can buy Jaguars instead of Chevrolets, and still not spend all their income or have enough time to enjoy all the things they have bought. Their **opportunity cost** of time is very high in part because they could earn a huge amount if they worked. It is also high because they have an abundance of goods to consume but no more time to spend consuming them than anyone else does.

Q: What would you do if you magically had two more hours per day? How would you spend the extra time? How would the things you buy change as a result of this time windfall?

1.22

Each semester after course grades were sent out I used to be deluged with phone calls and e-mail from students asking why they got the grades they did (always below what they expected). The answer usually was that they messed up on the final exam. A late colleague suggested a way of reducing this harassment. He pointed out that the students' **opportunity cost** is low after exam week and stays low until classes start the next semester. To discourage students from calling and e-mailing, he said that he writes on the exam that no complaints about grades will be acknowledged until the second week of the next semester. At that time students' opportunity cost of time is higher: They have better things to do, including attending their new classes. Only students who are deeply bothered by what they thought was unfair grading are willing to incur the high cost of inquiring. His suggestion has succeeded in sharply reducing the number of inquiries I receive.

Q: How does this policy treat students differently by year in school (freshman, sophomore, etc.), by the number of courses they are taking, and in other ways?

CHAPTER 2

Supply and Demand Curves

2.1

On a cold January day when our older son was five years old he came into the house with an ice-covered rock, probably a small piece of cement. He asked me, "Daddy, would you buy this for ten cents?" I said no, that was too much money for this particular rock. He then said, "Maybe you'll buy it for five cents." I said yes. Even though the rock was really ugly, I was pleased that our five-year-old son understood that **demand curves** slope downward and was willing to cut his price to sell his product.

> *Q: Offer to sell a much younger sibling, cousin, niece, or nephew ballpoint pens or CDs that you think might interest him or her. Start off with a high price and then work your way down. (This is like what we call a Dutch auction.) See if you can trace out the equivalent of a downward-sloping demand curve.*

2.2

Another bad night's sleep! Perhaps that's because my wage is too high. Sleep takes time, and time has value—its **opportunity cost.** Instead of sleeping I could be working and earning a wage. A study of the economics of sleep a number of years ago showed that higher-wage people sleep less. Your wage is the price of sleep, and there is a downward-sloping **demand curve** for sleep. The demand curve shifts with other characteristics: Having young kids at home reduces the amount of sleep people get, especially women. Additional nonwage income—inheritances and gifts—has small positive effects on sleep time, and people say that if they had more hours in the day, extra sleep is one of the top three things they would do with that extra time. Because time is scarce (there will always be only twenty-four hours in a day), the amount we sleep requires economic decision making.

> *Q: If your long-lost relative suddenly left you $1 million, would you sleep more or less? If somehow you were granted an extra two hours per day, how much extra per day would you sleep? What else would you do with the two hours?*

2.3

October 9, 2001—Has the entire travel-related industry been hurt by the terrorists? Not all, and this illustrates the point that goods and time must be combined. I had a long layover Sunday night in the Dallas–Fort Worth airport. I had never noticed, since I had never had a long layover like that, that there is a barbershop around Gate C20. I needed a haircut and went in and got one. The barber said that business has been booming since about one week after the September 11 terrorist attacks—much better business than ever before. The shoeshine man nearby said the same thing. More waiting time in airports seems to generate an increased demand for haircuts and shoeshines there.

> *Q: The issue here is that at various points in one's daily activities time seems to be wasted. What activities have you done— what goods have you bought—because you were stuck somewhere with nothing to do?*

2.4

I took my watch in to have the battery replaced. The jewelry store clerk said they could do it but would not be able to have it back until two days later. They could not do it any faster. Indeed, that seems to be very common: There are not that many activities in which things can be speeded up if you pay more. Why not? Surely for a higher price stores would be willing to provide services more rapidly, to let you get ahead in the "line" if you are willing to pay more. The **supply curve** should slope upward.

> *Q: List some reasons why the speeded-up market is not available. How would the supply-demand situation in the market for*

speeded-up service be different if I lived in a small town? An extremely big city?

2.5

We lived in the North all our lives and used to love to go to the Caribbean in the winter. Since moving to Texas nine years ago we have not gone at all. Today an old friend from the North suggested a reunion with other old friends in the Virgin Islands next December. We'd like to see all of these friends, but we have no real interest in going to the Caribbean. Have our tastes for Caribbean vacations changed, thus shifting our **demand curve**? *No!* The good being demanded is not Caribbean vacations but rather the pleasure of being in a warm climate. We get that pleasure every winter living in Texas, so why travel 2,000 miles for still more of it? Tastes don't change in most cases if we properly define the good that is being demanded.

> *Q: Assume you believe that Caribbean vacations combine two goods: pleasure from warm weather and gorgeous beaches. What happens to the demand for a Caribbean vacation by someone living in Texas if the vacation combines both of these goods?*

2.6

A news story mentioned the fact that the percentage of people cremated in the United States has risen from 3 percent to nearly 30 percent in the last quarter century. A spokesperson for the funeral directors association attributed this tremendous increase to the increased mobility of the American population: If you live far away from Grandpa and will not be visiting his grave, why not put him in an urn instead of in the ground? Does the rapid growth of cremation represent a shift in demand, as the spokesperson implies? Or does it instead represent people's substituting away from a product (burials) that has risen rapidly in price? It's difficult to tell: The quantity (of cremations) transacted can shift both because the demand has increased and because the price of its close **substitutes** has risen a lot. It is worth noting that no industry spokesperson is ever going to claim that a shift has occurred because consumers have responded to relative changes in price—to the rising price of burials. These people always argue that some factor beyond the industry members' control has caused the change. Price matters, but businesses don't want consumers to be reminded of that *except* when a business cuts prices.

> *Q: If funeral directors got together and agreed to raise the price of a cremation to equal that of a burial, how would that affect the demand curve for cremations?*

2.7

Economics textbooks say that the purpose of advertising is to provide the consumer with information, to shift **demand curves** outward and make markets work better. To some extent it serves that function. A lot of advertising, though, contains half-truths designed to lure the customer. A radio ad for a medical practice that performs laser eye surgery claimed, "Our doctors are trained at Princeton, Harvard, and Johns Hopkins." I'm sure that their docs went to Harvard or Johns Hopkins medical schools, but since Princeton has no medical school, the fact that a doctor got a nonmedical degree there tells me nothing about how competent that doctor is. The medical practice is using Princeton's luster to make its doctors' skills appear more attractive to consumers, even when that luster is irrelevant in regard to a doctor's surgical abilities. This is not quite false advertising, but it isn't providing any useful information to the consumer.

> *Q: If you were constructing an advertising campaign for this laser-surgery clinic, how would you try to "sell" the services of its doctors without providing misleading information?*

2.8

How do you decide which movies to pay to see, which books to read, and so forth? What shapes our **demand curves** for very particular products? The decisions depend on tastes, but partly also on the information you acquire about the movies or books. The problem is deciding what source of information to use. There are too many reviews and too many friends offering advice to pay attention to them all. Typically we acquire the information from people we trust, people whose past recommendations have proved valuable. I listen to movie reviewers who have done well for me in the past. This creates tremendous inertia: It's hard for a new reviewer or friend's comments to affect my thinking. Only if I'm suddenly short of advice might I spend the time paying attention to a new reviewer and perhaps listening to his or her advice. It's also hard to ditch familiar reviewers who've done well in the past, but it does happen. For years we chose movies on the basis of (the late) Siskel and Ebert recommendations. One New Year's Eve we went to a movie that Ebert claimed was the best of the year, *Breaking the Waves*. This painfully boring piece lasted three and a half hours, totally spoiling our evening. Since then we have paid no attention to Ebert's recommendations: With the big shock of his disastrous recommendation, he moved out of the group of information providers whom we spend our scarce time paying attention to when we make our choices.

> *Q: Who is likely to exhibit more inertia in using information about movies, books, and so on, someone age eighteen or someone age fifty-eight? Give an economic reason for your answer.*

2.9

A local store selling Mexican antiques, art, and furniture is running an advertisement: "We heard on the news that the recession is over. But that's no reason not to have a sale, so we're having our first and hopefully last 'end of recession' sale—all furniture 10 percent to 30 percent off." The ad does two things. Like many other ads, it announces a cut in prices designed to move the customer down the **demand curve.** More important, though, it makes clear that the price cut is both temporary and unlikely to be repeated; this is the "hopefully last" such sale. The store is trying to get customers to believe that prices will never be this low again. It's trying to shift demand from the future to the present as well as to induce customers to buy because prices are low.

> *Q: If everybody believes the ad, why doesn't everybody race to the store and quickly buy out its entire stock?*

2.10

During a stay in Russia in 1993 my wife and I went to the Maryinsky Theater in Saint Petersburg, where many of the most well-known ballets in the repertoire premiered. Among them is *Swan Lake*, which was playing on a Thursday night. We went to the theater, bargained for tickets outside the theater just before the show, and got great seats for only $7.50 per seat. On Saturday night we went back and decided to bargain for tickets to see *Legends of Love*, not a major work. The best price we could get was $20 per seat, barely low enough to persuade us to see the ballet. Why the difference? There were very few tourists early that June, and Russian workers typically don't go out much during the week. On Saturday Russians were competing for the tickets along with the few tourists. What shifted the **demand curve** wasn't what was playing but when it was showing.

> *Q: If you were planning programs for the Maryinsky Theater and wanted to get the most **revenue** for the theater, would you put the popular ballets on weekdays, as in this case, or the mediocre ones?*

2.11

Last week's *Economist* had a graph relating an index of corruption in a country to the amount of foreign investment per capita in that country. Independent agencies create measures of corruption to guide foreign investors. More corruption implies that the return to investing in a country—payoffs to greedy officials and the risk of having the investment confiscated—is lower. At any rate of return more corruption will reduce the amount of foreign investment funds supplied to an economy, because investors fear their funds will be confiscated and the return on investment will be lowered. That's exactly what happens: The most corrupt countries receive the smallest amounts of foreign investment: The supply curve for investment goods in a country slopes upward in the rate of return on investments. A good way for a poor country to attract more investment from abroad is to make itself attractive by not requiring bribes and payoffs.

> *Q: Draw supply curve and **demand curve** for foreign investment in light of this vignette. Be extra careful as you define what the price is and what determines the location of the supply curve.*

2.12

A rerun of *Law and Order* involved gang warfare in Manhattan. A New Jersey gang had been encroaching on the turf of a Manhattan gang's drug-selling operation. A number of murder victims had been found: people who did not seem like gang members. It turned out that the victims had formerly been customers of the Manhattan gang but had begun buying from the New Jersey gang. The murders were designed to scare other customers away from buying from the New Jerseyites and back to buying from the Manhattan gang—to shift demand curves in the two markets. If you can't advertise your product publicly, one way to encourage customers to buy from you instead of from your competitors is by convincing them that the price of buying from the competitor might be death. A murder threat adds greatly to the price of a product and probably has a profound effect on consumers' demand.

Q: What else might shift a consumer's demand curve for drugs sold by a particular gang?

2.13

According to Roman legend, a series of prophecies by the god Apollo were written down in nine books and interpreted by the Sibyl of Cumae (an old woman living in a cave whose interpretations were sought on numerous occasions by Roman leaders). Around 500 B.C. the Sibyl gave the Roman king Tarquinius Superbus a chance to buy the books for a price payable in gold. He refused. According to myth, the Sibyl burned three of the books and offered the king the remaining six for the original price she had asked for the nine. He refused again; she burned three more books and offered him the remaining three at the same price she had asked for all nine. This time he paid her. Why would he do that? How can his behavior be seen as consistent with the theory of consumer demand? By reducing the number of books in existence, the Sibyl made it clear to him that the remaining ones were now *scarcer*. She changed the quality of the product in the king's mind, which induced him to pay a price three times higher per book than he would have paid if he had bought the books at the original price.

*Q: Are there other examples where sellers destroy some of their product in order to enhance the value of what remains by so much as to increase their total **revenue**? Why don't we see very many other sellers behaving like the Sibyl and trying to convince people how valuable their product is by throwing some of it away?*

2.14

April 1, 2002—Tony Blair, the British prime minister, is visiting President Bush at the ranch at Crawford (near Waco), Texas, next weekend. A related fact is that radio and TV stations in the Waco area have raised their advertising rates substantially for the weekend. The facts are related because the demand for radio and TV advertising time depends on the number of "impressions" an ad is likely to make. With the influx of security and media people and the English-speaking world's focus on Waco for a few days, potential advertisers are more interested than usual in advertising because the potential audience is bigger. The **demand curve** for advertising has shifted out, and the local media outlets have sensibly decided to raise the price of their product.

Q: Draw the demand curve for radio advertising time in Waco, carefully labeling the axes and showing what is held constant along the curve.

2.15

April 5, 2002—The Costa Rican national election is in two days. Under national law no liquor can be sold today or tomorrow. This has put a real crimp in the entertainment activities of the younger participants in a conference I'm attending here. They like going out to discos, and they like drinking at discos. Discos and alcohol are **complements.** Because the price of alcohol is essentially infinite today—it can't be purchased—the demand for places at discos is way down. The local disco shut down at eleven PM tonight, much earlier than usual. When the election is over I expect a boom in disco action—and in drinking in discos.

*Q: What would happen to the demand for discos during this period if in addition to outlawing liquor sales the government temporarily legalized the use of marijuana? Draw the **demand curves** for the vignette and then for the scenario in this question.*

2.16

Johnson and Johnson (J&J), the giant pharmaceutical company, is running television ads promoting nursing as a rewarding career (and has even created a website, www.discovernursing.com).

This would seem like a charitable public-service campaign, but I'm skeptical. If it is successful, the ad campaign will induce more people to enter nursing, reducing the nursing shortage and/or lowering nurses' equilibrium wages. Along with nursing and other services, J&J's drug products make up the cost of medical care; they are **complements** in producing medical care. If one input becomes cheaper, costs and eventually the price of medical services fall. That fall in turn generates a rise in the amount of medical care demanded. It may be cynical, but J&J's apparently **altruistic** action can be viewed as an indirect way of raising the amount of its own product that is demanded.

> *Q: Graph **supply** and **demand curves** in the markets for nurses and J&J products before and after J&J undertakes its successful advertising campaign.*

2.17

On the *Tonight Show* Jay Leno mentioned that a plastic surgeon in Los Angeles was offering a discount on breast implants for Mother's Day. This doesn't seem to make any economic sense: Nobody will give this present to his or her mother, and Mother's Day is hardly associated with this surgical procedure. The holiday may be only an advertising convenience. The issue is more likely that **demand curves** shift to the left in the late springtime. People do not want to have cosmetic surgery that will inhibit them from walking around with little clothing, and the swimsuit season is almost here. By offering a discount the surgeon can keep his office busy at a time when the quantity transacted would otherwise be low.

> *Q: If this interpretation of the advertisement is correct, what other medical specialties would you expect to offer seasonal discounts, and why?*

2.18

A sign for sale in the local hardware store says, "Salesmen welcome—dog food is expensive." This clever sign operates in two markets. It raises the price of sales calls, thus reducing the number of salespeople who are likely to visit a house. It also makes the claim that salespeople and ordinary dog food are **substitutes** (in dogs' consumption). I don't know if dogs really view Alpo and door-to-door sellers as substitutes. (I doubt dogs view them as **complements**.) But as long as a few salespeople believe this, the sign accomplishes its purpose.

> *Q: Graph how the sign affects demand in the two markets discussed in the vignette.*

2.19

May 6, 2002—Tourism in Israel is way down, but hotels and other tourist facilities are doing their best to keep **revenue** up. One luxury hotel in Jerusalem is advertising that it will provide its guests with bulletproof vests. A similar, though less bizarre, attempt to shift demand is practiced in rainy winters by luxury hotels in San Francisco. Those hotels offer guests large umbrellas for use during the day when they leave the hotel. Are these clever strategies going to raise demand? They might be smart competitive moves: Those people who would come to Jerusalem or go to San Francisco in the winter anyway might feel safer or happier staying at these hotels than at their competitors. But for those potential guests who are not committed to visiting the city, seeing a hotel offering this "extra" could well reduce their demand.

> *Q: Which policy, offering bulletproof vests in Israel or offering umbrellas in San Francisco, is more likely to generate an increase in demand?*

CHAPTER 3

Supply and Demand Together— Unrestricted Markets

3.1

Teaching a class of 500 students introductory microeconomics is hurting my voice, and I've had to cut back on my cigar smoking. I am only one of many cigar smokers. But what if all Americans found out that cigar smoking hurts their voices? What would happen to the **equilibrium price** and **equilibrium quantity** in the cigar market in the United States? What would happen to the Cuban economy (some people do have access to illegal Cuban cigars)?

> *Q: Draw the supply-demand graphs implied by this vignette and trace the effects of the behavior that is implied. Then show in the graph what would happen in all the markets discussed here if the opposite occurred and the surgeon general announced, "Cigar smoking reduces cancer and is generally beneficial for health."*

3.2

September 15, 2001—Continental Airlines, in a press release, said it will immediately reduce its long-term flight schedule by approximately 20 percent and will be forced to furlough some 12,000 employees. The airline said the cutbacks "are a direct result of the current and anticipated adverse effects on the demand for air travel caused by this week's terrorist attacks on the United States and the operational and financial costs of dramatically increased security requirements." Continental clearly believes that there has been a shift in the **demand curve,** and its announcement indicates a movement down the supply schedule.

> *Q: Draw the supply-demand graph, labeling the axes carefully. What is the good or service being sold? What changed to shift the demand curve: income, tastes, prices of related goods, or what?*

3.3

September 20, 2001—How big should the airline bailout be? One way to think about it is to realize that the government-imposed shutdown, plus the fears of potential passengers, shifted the **demand curve** to the left and down the **supply curve.** This resulted in a reduction in **revenue.** Total revenue last year was about $125 billion, and so one week's shutdown cost $2.5 billion in lost revenue. Beyond that, we don't know how much the loss will be now that they've resumed flying. I don't think it will be very big after a few weeks. That being the case, President Bush's $5 billion bailout seems a lot more sensible than the immense sums the airlines are seeking.

> *Q: Instead of talking about airlines, let's say that students stop taking economics courses and universities and colleges fire as many economics professors as they can. Graph the supply-demand situation in the market (what is the good or service?) before and after the change. Using the graph, show how big a bailout the government should give to economics professors.*

3.4

A *News of the Weird* story reported that a pro-prostitution group is offering deals to help get teenage hookers off the streets. For a contribution of $150,000 the seven prostitutes on the committee promise to sleep with the donor (in Nevada). The story goes on to state, "Critics note that the campaign, ostensibly to save wayward children, would also result in less competition for the council's constituency." This can be viewed as two markets: one for adult prostitutes and one for teenage prostitutes. The two are probably not perfect **substitutes,** but the (adult) council members believe that by decreasing the supply of teenage prostitutes, they can shift the **demand curve** for their services and raise their **equilibrium price.**

> *Q: Draw the **demand** and **supply curves** in the two relevant markets: teenage and adult prostitutes. Draw the situation described in the vignette. Then draw what would happen if the services of teenagers and adults were **complements.***

3.5

October 3, 2001—If Barry Bonds hits a seventieth or, better still, a seventy-first home run, what is going to happen to the value of the ball that Mark McGwire hit for his seventieth home run in 1998 (for which someone paid $3 million at an auction)?

> *Q: After graphing the market for souvenir baseballs, assume that baseballs become less lively (less likely to be hit for a long distance), as some have argued they were in the past. What will this do to the value of souvenir home-run baseballs?*

3.6

A travel magazine at the airport had a story headlined: "Cheap vacations—why not Nebraska?" Without denigrating Nebraska too much, one might ask oneself why the vacations might be so cheap. The answer is probably that few people currently want to vacation there, so that land prices and other prices are very low. The **demand curve** is far to the left. It's cheap precisely because few people want to go there, so that as a tourist attraction it will be a bargain only for those who enjoy Nebraskan things.

> *Q: If you were the governor of Nebraska, what else would you do to encourage more people to visit the state? How would you represent the governor's effort in a supply-demand diagram?*

3.7

In the James Bond movie *Goldfinger* the main character, Auric Goldfinger, owns a huge horde of gold. The plot centers on his attempt to explode a nuclear device at Fort Knox, where the U.S. gold supply was housed at that time. He hatches this plot in order to irradiate the U.S. gold supply, rendering it valueless. His idea is that with the U.S. gold horde gone, the world **equilibrium price** of gold will rise. His wealth, which consists of the value of the gold he owns, will increase with no additional effort on his part.

> *Q: Analyze in a supply-demand graph the economics of Gold-finger's activities. What would happen in the market if after Gold-finger's success people decided that gold rings were not necessary mutual gifts to brides and grooms? [Extra credit, not economics: How long before the nuclear device was scheduled to explode did James Bond shut down its timer?]*

3.8

I've been doing more and more online shopping, making me part of a worldwide trend. It makes you think: What will this trend do to the price of land, a price in a related market? Certainly with online shopping there's less need to use space for retail outlets. The trend should produce general-equilibrium effects, reducing land prices. But also, since retail outlets are typically nearer to downtowns than to residences, this should flatten out the relationship between rents and distance from downtowns. This trend thus will especially help those who wish to build residential housing near downtowns, because land prices there will fall.

> *Q: What other markets will be affected if online shopping forces out more and more "regular" shopping? Graph the effects on price and quantity in those markets?*

3.9

December 9, 2001—Every Saturday in a Jewish synagogue a section out of the Five Books of Moses is read. The next weekend the portion includes Genesis 41:1–36, dealing with Joseph's interpretation of Pharaoh's dream, where Joseph tells Pharaoh to set aside one-fifth of the produce in the good years to tide the country over during the upcoming famine. This is a classic example of **speculation**: shifting supply from a time when supply is high to a time when it is low. The question is: Why one-fifth—why not more or less? Presumably Joseph had some idea of how much of the stored grain would deteriorate, how bad the famine would be, and how the Pharaoh valued the current consumption of his subjects compared to their future consumption. He must have chosen one-fifth by accounting for all these factors, since he was a pretty smart fellow.

> *Q: Graph the supply-demand situations in the good years and the bad years. Then show how Joseph's suggestion affects the markets in the two different times. Now show how the amount Joseph asked the Pharaoh to set aside will change if Joseph believes that a plague of rats might infest the stored grain. How would it change if Joseph believed that Egypt would have an influx of foreign purchasers (like his brothers) during the time of famine? Graph both cases.*

3.10

December 8, 2001—A story in *The Economist* talks about converting prices from the old currencies to the euro. For example, French people who attend mass typically throw a 10-franc coin (1.52 euros) into the collection plate. Will they round down and throw in a 1-euro coin or round up and throw in a 2-euro coin? The same "problem" exists throughout the economy. But is it a problem? Probably not. Presumably some prices will round up a bit, others down a bit, with the average unchanged, and some mass goers will give 1 euro, others 2, with the average the same.

> *Q: If you were one of the French mass attendees, what would you do? Think of this as a market for a good or service (what is the good or service being talked about?). Would the shift to euros shift your **demand curve**? Why or why not?*

3.11

December 28, 2001—An article in the local paper today reported on the hypocrisy of the Taliban. They bought raw opium at $1,000 a pound and then severely enforced restrictions on growing opium. The **equilibrium price** quickly rose to $4,000 a pound, and they then sold their horde of stored opium on the international market. For a group with relatively little secular education and one which is devoted to a command economy, they understood very well the nature of supply and demand.

> *Q: Graph the Taliban's policy in a supply-demand graph. What are the effects on its strategy if local opium growers attempt to produce illegal opium on their own?*

3.12

I went to buy a pair of running shoes today and asked if there were any half-price shoes. There were, but as always, there were none in my size. This happens to me at sales for all kinds of clothes: Lots of things are on sale, but never in my size. Usually there are very large or very small sizes on sale. I am of average height, and my clothing sizes are about average. Why am I always left out? The answer has to do with inventory theory: In sizes that are unusual stores will stock a higher supply of items relative to the average demand, since there is more variability in the average number of items bought each month. In the common sizes stores can predict better. When, as frequently happens, demand for unusual sizes is small, there are lots of unusual sizes left over compared to the number of potential buyers. Demand for standard sizes is very heavy, with relatively less variation, so that the number left over is small compared to the (large) number of potential buyers.

> *Q: Show the effect of computerized inventory policy and "just-in-time" manufacturing and delivery in the market for "leftover" goods. Show this in the market for goods bought by average-size people and then in the market for goods bought by people of unusual sizes.*

3.13

An advertisement for financial advice in the *Toronto Globe and Mail* shows a naked couple in bed making love. (This ad probably would not appear in an American newspaper.) Below the picture is a small banner with a stylized news report saying, "Sheer Inc. recalls 100,000 condoms." On the right side of the picture are three graphs: The first shows the stock price of Sheer Inc. falling as it moves out the *x* axis over time. The second shows the stock price of Cupid Condom Inc., presumably a **substitute** for Sheer Inc., rising as it moves out the *x* axis. The final graph shows sales of maternity wear, also substitutes for condoms, rising as they move out the *x* axis.

Q: *If you were drawing up a revision of this advertisement, what two extra graphs depicting additional markets would you put on the right side of the picture? In other words, what are some other related goods that would also be affected by the Sheer Inc. recall?*

3.14

January 15, 2002—A story in the local newspaper reported on the 17 percent salary increase (to $1.7 million per year) that our football coach is getting. The story went on to talk about the tremendous explosion in the salaries of head football coaches in NCAA Division I universities in the last several years. This has occurred even though there is no obvious increase in **revenues** generated from college football. The reason for the boom is that the market for professional football head coaches has increasingly become integrated with the college market, with a number of college coaches moving to the National Football League (NFL) (e.g., Spurrier to the Redskins for $5 million per year) and vice versa. Salaries in pro football are now spilling over into college football. College football has always been a subsidized training program for pro football, and now the coaching markets are becoming more integrated as well.

Q: *Show what would happen to the market for college coaches if the NCAA allowed schools to pay salaries to the college athletes they are training to play in the National Football League. What would happen to this market if people got tired of watching college football on television and instead spent more time watching the NFL on television?*

3.15

January 29, 2002—The headline in the local newspaper reads, "Central Texas had nation's widest gap between supply and demand [of office space] in '01." A graph in the story shows occupancy rates falling from 97 percent to 86 percent during the year. Another graph shows that the rental price per square foot had risen from $12 in 1991 to $26 in 2000 as this area boomed but had fallen to $24 in 2001. The problem will be heightened, so the story states, by the completion this year of one million square feet of additional office space—an outward shift in the **supply curve** at a time when the **demand curve** has shifted inward. If I were planning to rent office space and seeking bargains, I'd wait a few months.

> *Q: Given the state of this market, what would you do if you were leasing office space? What would you do if you were one of the people who had a new office building that could be completed in the next three months? What would you do if you had already dug a hole to build an office building but had not gone any further?*

3.16

At lunch we were talking about the fact that female porn stars are paid many times what male porn stars are paid. On the supply side the ability to fake a good performance is clearly greater for women than for men, and that should make women's pay lower. Also on the supply side, though, the number of men willing to enter this occupation may exceed the number of women. Clearly, supply is much less important than demand: The clientele consists almost exclusively of men who want to look at women and are willing to pay large premiums for what they view as attractive women. Most of the audience has little interest in looking at the men on the screen, and the men's wages reflect that.

> *Q: In his novel* The Wanting Seed *Anthony Burgess described a world in which homosexuality was encouraged and was much more common than heterosexuality. In such a world there would presumably still be pornography. How would the supply-demand situation and the relative wages of male and female porn stars be different compared to what they are in today's market?*

3.17

According to *The Economist,* Nigeria subsidizes oil to the tune of U.S. $2 billion per year. The neighboring countries do not have the same abundant supply of oil and do not offer any **subsidies** to consumers. Thus Nigeria, despite being a major producer of oil, has a shortage. Middlemen buy up domestic oil at the low, subsidized price and sell it in neighboring countries and elsewhere at the higher world price. The Nigerian government has subsidized an easily transportable commodity for which there is a world market that offers suppliers a higher price than the price the oil sells for in Nigeria.

> *Q: What if Nigeria instead produced coal and subsidized its price? Would the market for coal in Nigeria be affected the same way as the market for oil?*

3.18

A book I'm reading describes the reaction to Gutenberg's invention of the printing press in the 1450s by noting, "Professional copyists opposed it, . . . along with aristocrats who feared that their libraries would decrease in value" [Isacoff, *Temperament*. New York: Knopf, 2001]. It's nice to see that even in the fifteenth century people understood the impact of increases in supply on the wages of workers producing a **substitute** and on the **equilibrium price** in the market. It also makes one thankful for progress: We did not see huge protests from the producers of mechanical calculators when they were displaced by electronic ones or computers in the 1960s and 1970s or from watchmakers and watch repairers when quartz watches became popular at around the same time.

> *Q: Graph the market for copyists' services in the fifteenth century and show the impact of the invention of the printing press. Think of two other innovations that had similar effects in the market for workers with particular skills.*

3.19

A story in the *New York Times* discussed a problem in London: There has been a shortage of taxis on the streets in the evening and at night. There is no overall shortage of London cabs. The problem has been that drivers don't want to work evenings and nights. The solution: The city government has raised the regulated rates for evening-night cab fares to about 30 percent above daytime fares. This has encouraged a 20 percent increase in the number of drivers who are willing to switch from day work. Is this increase big enough? The fare increase will reduce the number of cab trips demanded too. Unless the shortage was immense—more than 20 percent excess demand—we can expect the initial large increase in the supply of cabbies to be excessive. Passengers should have no trouble finding cabs, and cabbies will be complaining about insufficient demand.

> *Q: Graph the situation in this market before and after the night-time fares were raised. Show the new price in relation to the equilibrium in this market if the new fare is too high.*

3.20

There's a $1 surcharge for downtown taxi rides during rush hour in Washington, DC. This is somewhat like the previous vignette but different: This is a fixed dollar amount; that was a percentage surcharge. As with the London surcharge, the purpose is to *increase the amount supplied* (in Washington, during a time of peak demand). Why is the surcharge a fixed amount in Washington and a percentage in London when the purposes are so similar? The reason is that fares in Washington are also fixed: You pay the same amount for any taxi ride within the downtown zone, no matter what the distance. In London the fare is metered by distance. At first glance it looks like the surcharges create different incentives, but coupled with each town's basic pricing structure, they create similar incentives. Both function as percentage increases in taxi fares.

> *Q: As a result of this surcharge in rush hours, what will happen to the **equilibrium price** and equilibrium quantity for taxi rides outside rush hours?*

3.21

March 16, 2002—Only six months after the September 11 terrorist attacks there's a truly depressing sight in U.S. airports: American flag paraphernalia is now discounted heavily. (In the local airport a sign reads, "All patriotic T-shirts now $4.99.") Have Americans already forgotten those recent events? I doubt it, although the initial explosion of demand for these souvenirs has passed. Suppliers, anxious to meet what they saw was a tremendous shortage of patriotic clothing, geared up production lines and increased the *amount supplied* to meet the huge *increase in demand.* Some of them overshot the mark, leading to temporary surpluses once the initial increase in demand had been satisfied.

> *Q: By April 21 the same place was advertising, "All patriotic T-shirts now $2.99." Does this change surprise you?*

3.22

The U.S. government subsidizes cattle grazers to use federally owned lands (mostly in the West). The average price per month per animal unit is around $1.50. Private landowners charge around $11 per month per animal unit on their lands; the free-market price is around $11 per month. Does that mean that the **subsidy** is $9.50 per month? *No*—it's more than that. The federal subsidy induces cattle grazers to use federal lands. That shifts their demand away from private lands. The federal subsidy lowers the **equilibrium price** on private lands below what would prevail if there were no subsidy. In an unsubsidized market demand for grazing private lands would be higher, resulting in an equilibrium price above $11.

> *Q: Graph the market **supply** and **demand curves** for grazing on federal and private lands. Show the effect of the subsidy to grazing on federal lands on the prices observed in each market and then show what would happen if the subsidy were removed.*

3.23

A story in today's local newspaper about declining personal computer (PC) prices states, "As a general rule, the supply of parts needed to build computers exceeds the demand, and prices decline steadily. Steady improvements in performance also push down prices for existing technology." These sentences are garbled economics. It's true that PC prices have declined steadily. That's not because supply always exceeds demand but instead because technical improvements keep shifting **supply curves** outward, reflecting firms' ability to offer PCs profitably at lower prices. It's not a matter of continual disequilibrium but instead that the **equilibrium price** keeps changing as technology improves. Also, how could "steady improvements in performance" be compatible with "existing technology"? They're not; the story is again describing the process of technological improvements driving down input (parts) costs and steadily *increasing the supply* of PCs.

> *Q: Draw the **supply** and **demand curves** in the market for computer parts. Show how these curves have shifted over time, carefully indicating what has happened to the equilibrium price and quantity sold.*

3.24

The General Manager of WDIV-TV in Detroit editorialized on air this week about rising gasoline prices. He was particularly annoyed that gas prices seem to rise around holiday weekends. I would be very unhappy if they didn't rise then. Demand is high on those weekends, and the storage capacity of gasoline stations is limited. If prices didn't rise, the amount demanded would be even higher, and we would observe temporary shortages of gasoline and a lot of unhappy drivers. The high price around holidays is what keeps supply and demand in balance.

> *Q: Graph the unrestricted equilibrium in the market for gasoline before a holiday. Then show what would happen if gas station owners listened to the general manager and held the price constant in response to the shock of a holiday weekend.*

3.25

May 9, 2002—Airlines have had frequent-flyer programs for twenty years. The stock of unredeemed frequent-flyer mileage is like consumer income. It is used in the market for a limited number of seats to "buy" "free tickets" on the airline. The amount of unredeemed mileage has more than doubled in the last five years, while the "price" of a seat—25,000 miles on American Airlines, for example—has not changed. During the recession the market demand for paid airline tickets has been low, and the airlines have kept the supply of seats set aside for free tickets unchanged and have not altered the "price." As the economy recovers, the **demand** curve by paying customers will shift outward, and airlines will maximize profits by reducing the supply of free seats to frequent flyers. At that time a shortage will begin to exist in the market for free seats. Either holders of mileage will find it increasingly difficult to obtain tickets for travel at the times they want or the airlines will raise the price of a free ticket to equilibrate the rising demand and the reduced supply.

Q: Draw the market for free seats before the growth in unredeemed mileage. Then show how that growth has shifted demand in that market. Then show the market during and after the recession.

CHAPTER 4

Supply and Demand—
Restricted Markets

4.1

Several years ago Cambridge, Massachusetts, was forced by a statewide referendum to end its rent control program. Rent controls are a **price ceiling** on apartment rentals. Their removal created a free market for the over one-third of the Cambridge housing stock whose rents had been controlled. Not surprisingly, rental prices rose very rapidly. Owners had not been making repairs to their housing, but freeing up the rents generated a boom in investment in improving the housing stock: Building permits increased 50 percent. Removing the restrictions on this market produced exactly the results that economic thinking would predict: higher prices, but higher quality too. Since the city relies on property taxes, freeing up the housing market also generated an increase in property tax funds flowing into the city's coffers.

> *Q: Draw a supply-demand graph describing the Cambridge housing market before and after the removal of rent controls.*

4.2

October 28, 2001—There's a highly successful new presentation of *The Producers*, the old Mel Brooks movie, on Broadway. Rather than let scalpers make money by reselling regular tickets at outlandish prices, the theater has set aside fifty seats to be sold at $475 apiece starting a few days before each performance. This way the theater and those who finance the show make money from its popularity (from the shortage normally created by the low price and the fixed supply of seats).

> *Q: Does this policy make sense for new, untried shows? What will be the effects of this policy if show goers believe that it will be standard policy for all Broadway shows that are typically sold out?*

4.3

My visiting eighty-three-year-old mother told the assembled family one of the oldest economics jokes under the sun. A lady went into a butcher shop and asked, "How much is the ground beef?" "It's $2.95 a pound," responded the butcher. "That's outrageous," said the lady. "The other butcher shop in town advertises it for $1.79 a pound." "Yes," said the butcher, "and I have it even cheaper than that when I also don't have it in stock." Telling customers that an item is priced very low when in fact none is in stock may be a good way of getting them into the store, but it will leave them unhappy because their **demand** exceeds the storekeeper's available supply.

> *Q: Think about the market for labor instead of the market for ground beef. What does this joke tell you about the effect on the demand for low-skilled labor of proposals to set the **minimum wage** in the United States at $10 per hour?*

4.4

The association meetings I just attended function as a job market for professors; colleges try to hire new Ph.D.s for teaching jobs. Universities rent hotel suites at the meeting and interview the students there. In the last few years the interviewers have included many colleges from Europe, and students from European universities have begun attending and interviewing for U.S. jobs too. This internationalization of the job market has resulted in increased **demand** for interviewing suites in hotels, and those suites are in very short **supply**. The secretary of the association tells me that henceforth he will be negotiating contracts with hotels that allow them to charge more than in the past for suites while continuing to use the money to allow individuals to attend the meetings and stay in highly subsidized hotel rooms. Not a bad way to react to an increased shortage.

Q: What will this policy do to attendance at the meetings by job interviewers and by students looking for jobs?

4.5

A story in today's local paper comments on the teacher "shortage" and notes that one-fourth of the elementary and secondary schoolteachers hired in Texas last year were not fully certified. Math, science, and foreign languages vacancies were especially hard to fill with certified teachers. These are the subjects in which good jobs are available outside teaching. There is a common pay scale in teaching, independent of the subject: Teachers with the same experience and the same education receive the same pay regardless of their specialty. The common pay scale operates as a **price ceiling**. It guarantees that the shortages will be especially severe in areas where potential teachers have better outside alternatives.

Q: If you could offer different pay for elementary and secondary schoolteachers in different subjects, what signs would tell you whether you had the pay scale set correctly?

4.6

A story in *The Economist* talks about an attempt in Hong Kong to lower the **minimum wage** of live-in maids (most are from the Philippines). The problem is that the Hong Kong middle class is feeling the effects of a recession. At the current minimum wage some families claim they cannot afford to employ their maids anymore. With this leftward shift in **demand** and a fixed wage, the result will be that some maids will lose their jobs. Lowering the minimum wage will enable employers to keep the maids, but it will also ensure that all maids will receive lower monthly pay. The choice about policy is thus very simple: Keep the minimum wage up and reduce maids' employment opportunities (and opportunities for Hong Kong residents to have maids to take care of their children) or cut the minimum wage, keeping employment up but lowering each employed maid's earnings. Because of the reduced demand in Hong Kong, the amount that the maids remit to their families in the Philippines will drop, reducing income and spending in that country. Regardless of the policy choices made in Hong Kong, the recession in Hong Kong will spill over to the Philippines.

> *Q: Show the effect of firing the maids, or lowering their wages, on the market for televisions in the Philippines. Show the effect on the market for factory workers in Japan (where many televisions are made).*

4.7

February 13, 2002—This week's *Economist* talks about a shortage of money—not like when I don't have enough bills in my pocket to pay for lunch but when a whole country is short of paper money. West Africa has its money printed by the same firms that print euros. Those companies have been running at capacity printing euros for the changeover in the European Union and have not been printing enough African francs, especially smaller bills. While the shortage is temporary and should have been foreseen and avoided, it has led people to spend time trying to find ways around it. In some cases people have been paying a premium for smaller bills, giving someone a larger bill in exchange for smaller bills worth less in total. This "price" of the scarce smaller bills helps to bring the market for them back into equilibrium.

> *Q: Could this kind of temporary shortage ever happen in the United States? If small bills were scarce, how would you pay for small items?*

4.8

At lunch today someone mentioned a large "gentleman's club" (in Texas that means a topless bar) that is near a shopping center here and pointed out how successful it is. Someone else expressed surprise that there are very few bars with a naked wait staff in Austin. There's a very simple reason: State law allows selling alcohol by the drink in topless bars but not in others, and it is the sale of alcohol that generates profits for the bars. Bottomless clubs might well be preferred by many customers, but because they are not profitable under the restrictions imposed by state law, what customers probably view as an inferior **substitute** is much more widespread.

> *Q: What would happen in the market for such venues if the state repealed the law allowing liquor sales only in topless bars? What would happen if the state passed a law outlawing tobacco use in all of these bars?*

4.9

At my favorite southwestern cuisine restaurant the prices of entrees are much higher than they were a year ago. At 6:30 PM there were still some empty tables. In past years, the place was completely packed and a long line was already forming by 6:15 PM. I pointed out to a colleague how sensitive people's demand to price is even in the case of good restaurant meals. He asked, "Are you sure it's that, or has the *demand* shifted because of the recession?" Good point—a decline in quantity sold could result from either cause. Merely observing that there has been a reduction in the equilibrium quantity doesn't tell us whether we are moving up a **demand curve** or whether the demand has shifted left. I don't know, but in this case I think I'm right. If the recession were the cause, why would the restaurant have gone ahead and raised prices? The higher prices reflect a decision to seek a less price-conscious clientele: to raise **revenue** by moving up a nearly vertical demand curve. Unsurprisingly, this was the first time at this restaurant that the management was happy to let the customers linger over dinner.

> *Q: Would the restaurant management have been more or less likely to raise prices if, instead of a recession, the area had been in an economic boom? In that case, would the management have been as willing to let customers eat a leisurely dinner?*

4.10

One of the favorite souvenirs in my office is a set of my grandpa's leftover gasoline *ration* coupons from World War II. These coupons, without which U.S. drivers could not buy gasoline during

the war years, accompanied money in the purchase of this product: You needed a coupon and, for example, a quarter to buy a
gallon of gasoline. By issuing coupons the federal government
both guaranteed that civilians had access to a fixed **supply** of
gasoline and ensured that civilians in war-essential jobs had the
opportunity to buy more than other civilians could. The system
did not work badly, so my parents tell me, but would it work as
well today? Actually, if the coupons could be traded, it probably
would work better now. Markets, aided by computerized trad-
ing, would quickly spring up, and the coupons would very
quickly wind up in the hands of those citizens who value them
most at the margin rather than those who were fortunate enough
to receive them. But if that were true, why give out the coupons
in the first place? Why not just let the free market determine who
gets the gasoline?

> *Q: What are the differences between what would happen in a free
> market and what would happen if tradable coupons had to be used?*

4.11

March Madness—The NCAA basketball tournament usually
offers great examples of economic behavior, since tickets to the
games (especially the final sixteen matches) are sold in markets
with tremendous excess **demand**. The Midwest Regional in 2000
was held in Michigan, where ticket scalping is illegal. Worse still,
the police were serious about enforcing the antiscalping ordi-
nances. Ticket scalpers got around the police and the restrictions
in a very clever way. If you wanted to buy the best ticket available, you could buy it from a scalper at the same price he or she
paid, but you also were forced to buy a map of the arena to show
you where the seat was, and the map was priced at $1,000! This
equilibrated the market—the full price of the ticket, including the
outrageously priced map, was just enough to eliminate any
excess demand.

> *Q: Have you ever bought a ticket for a sporting event or concert
> for more than the face value of the ticket? Would it have made any
> difference to you if you had been charged the same amount but
> part of the total cost was for a map, some popcorn, two "free
> drinks," or something else?*

4.12

We exchanged our excellent second row center mezzanine seats to the opera tomorrow night for seats tonight at the same price but higher up and way off to one side. Why were these seats priced the same? How does the opera company decide which season ticket holder gets the better seats within each section? It would be too complicated to charge large numbers of different prices depending on individual rows, center or side, and so on. The costs of administering that system would be too great. Instead, there are only a few prices, none of which represents the single **equilibrium price,** with customers allocated within the section partly based on first-come, first-served, and partly based on the size (if any) of each customer's money contribution to the opera company. The contribution functions as an additional price that removes the disequilibrium resulting from the small number of different prices. This kind of pricing is widespread: For fifteen years we had tickets on the five-yard line, high upper deck, for the Michigan State University football season. We never moved closer to the fifty-yard line or farther down. Big Ten rules and the same administrative costs that caused the opera company's behavior prevented the athletic department from charging different prices in the faculty section. It was well known that generous contributions guaranteed better seats.

> *Q: Student seats at college football games are allocated by lottery at many schools. Why don't the schools allocate the better student seats the same way as seats for the faculty, by giving better seats to students who contribute to the athletic program?*

4.13

Places at Czech universities are limited; the **supply curve** is vertical. Rather than charging tuition for this scarce good, the universities base admission on competitive exams. The entrance exams include tests on Czech history and language. Because the universities are quite good by Eastern European standards, many Russian high school students would like to attend. In the United States these "out-of-state" students would be allowed in but would pay very high tuition. Charging tuition isn't possible in the Czech Republic. Instead, lucrative businesses have arisen that offer training in the Czech language and history to foreign students seeking to do well on the entrance exams and be admitted to Czech universities. Even though the universities create a **shortage** of places by keeping tuition low, the market has created a product—the entry training courses—that essentially functions as part of the price foreigners pay to go to Czech universities. Unfortunately, the universities receive none of the **revenue**.

> *Q: What would happen to the market for entry-exam training if the Czech government allowed universities to charge higher tuition to noncitizens?*

4.14

During much of the semester my four weekly office hours are nearly empty. The students who show up then get a lot of individualized attention: There is a **surplus** in the market for my office hours. In the week before each midterm office hours are jammed, with long lines of students seeking help and being urged to finish quickly: There is a **shortage** of office hours. What can be done to solve the peak-load problem, in which the supply is fixed but the demand varies greatly over the semester? Unless I spent thirty office hours in each midterm week, I would be unable to satisfy all the students. The best solution is advertising to shift demand from peak to slack times. Early in the semester the students are told about this problem. The clever ones shift their visits to the previously slack times and hope to benefit more from their time in my office. It helps, but there is still a shortage right before exams and a surplus most of the time.

> *Q: Economists believe in using prices to eliminate disequilibriums in markets. If the professor could charge the students for office-hour visits, do you have any suggestions on how prices might be used to remove or at least reduce this problem? Are there any other nonmonetary incentives that the professor might use?*

4.15

CNN reports that the Hawaii legislature is considering putting a ceiling on the price of gasoline (although it wouldn't become effective until 2004). If they impose a ceiling of $3 a gallon, it won't matter; it will be an ineffective **price ceiling.** But if they are serious and impose a ceiling that is effective—say, $1.75 per gallon, which is below the current **equilibrium price**—they will cause serious problems for the state. With a price ceiling that low, suppliers of gasoline, especially refiners that have the choice of not shipping to the islands, will withhold the product, since they won't be able to make a profit on it. For residents this will make commuting more difficult. For tourists the difficulty of finding gasoline will make Hawaii a less attractive destination. While it may make some residents feel good, this proposal will hurt the Hawaiian economy.

> *Q: If they impose the price ceiling and a war in the Middle East disrupts oil supplies, what will happen in the Hawaiian market compared to the market for gasoline on the mainland?*

4.16

As part of the terms for ending the 1991 Gulf War the United Nations required Iraq to sell its oil to intermediaries at a fixed price. Investigations have shown that Iraq has added small surcharges to the fixed price and has used the **revenue** to finance a rebuilding of Saddam Hussein's war machine. Why are buyers willing to pay the surcharges? Simply because the fixed price is below the market price of oil; it is a **price ceiling** that makes Iraqi oil a bargain without the surcharges. The surcharges serve to equilibrate the market for oil. Unfortunately, because they are secret, they can be siphoned off for Saddam's nefarious purposes. If the United Nations simply bought the oil at the market price, it would be much easier to police where the oil revenues go and make sure they are not used to rebuild Iraq's military.

> *Q: If the United Nations paid the market price, what would be the level of surcharges that Iraq would be able to add to the price of the oil it sells?*

CHAPTER 5

The Consumer— Incentives and Elasticities

5.1

The easiest example to use to understand elasticity is the behavior of the Cookie Monster on *Sesame Street*. As nearly every American under the age of thirty-five knows, the Cookie Monster (CM) eats only cookies. Assume that his income is $100 per week and that the price of a cookie is $1. If the price doubles, he cuts his consumption in half; the amount that he spends on cookies stays constant at $100. This means that CM's **price elasticity of demand** for cookies is exactly −1. His demand is **unit-elastic.** If the price is $1 and his weekly income doubles to $200, he doubles the number of cookies he buys. That means that CM's **income elasticity of demand** for cookies is +1. For him, cookies are neither a **luxury** nor a **necessity** but are on the very thin border in between.

> *Q: Are pretzels **substitutes** or **complements** for cookies to the Cookie Monster?*

5.2

Every year I do a survey of my students to see if their demand for places at the university responds to prices. The price of places at the university is the tuition charged. I offer students the possibility of zero tuition increase for next year, a 5 percent increase for next year, and a 10 percent increase. Each student is then asked whether he or she will return next year. I recently got the following results: For a 5 percent tuition increase the number of students returning would decrease by 2.2 percent, implying a **price elasticity of demand** equaling −.44. For a 10 percent tuition increase, however, the number returning would fall by 11.8 percent, implying an elasticity of −1.18. The **demand curve** is surely downward-sloping. Not only does the number of places demanded decline when tuition rises more; the responsiveness of demand—the price elasticity of demand—is greater in percentage terms when the university tries to raise tuition by higher amounts. That's not surprising: **Substitutes** that suddenly become slightly cheaper don't affect behavior proportionately as much as substitutes that suddenly become relatively a lot cheaper.

> *Q: Ask yourself the same question. List tuition increases for your school for next year and ask how many of you and your friends are planning to return. Are your freshman friends more or less likely to return than your friends who are juniors?*

5.3

A young woman gets pregnant and decides to abort rather than bear the child. You would think that this is a highly personal decision in which economics couldn't play a role. Even in something as personal as this, though, prices and incomes seem to matter. A study of changes in interstate differences in abortions shows that where and when the price of an abortion is higher, the number of abortions is lower. The **price elasticity of demand** is around −1: The demand for abortions is essentially **unit-elastic.** At the same price, abortions are more common in those states and those times where incomes are higher: The **income elasticity of demand** for abortions is around +.5. Abortion is a **superior good,** but it is a **necessity**, not a **luxury**.

> *Q: Take another delicate procedure: liver transplants. Would you think the demand for liver transplants is more or less price-elastic than the demand for abortions? Explain your reasoning.*

5.4

September 24, 2001—On National Public Radio this morning a representative of the airline industry said that if the prices drop a bit, we'll see a rush of ticket buying. The question is: Is the **price elasticity of demand** sufficiently high to overcome the shift in

demand that has taken place because of the terror? Also, is that shift very short term, or is it longer term because of the increased waiting times caused by security checks and the reminders of problems as flights are delayed to pull off passengers who are wanted in connection with the September 11 attacks?

> *Q: Assume that there has been no drop in demand. How elastic would the **demand curve** have to be for a 10 percent drop in prices to increase the airlines' **revenues** above what they were before? Now answer the same question assuming that demand has dropped by 10 percent.*

5.5

During class a number of students were amused when they thought I had made an obscene gesture while pointing to something on the overhead. I hadn't, but it reminded me of a story. In spring 2000 I was taking a taxi from a conference center in rural Bavaria, Germany, to the Munich airport. Another driver did something really stupid, and I told the taxi driver that in the United States I would have given that obscene gesture. He said he would too, but there's a fine of 500 deutschmarks (about $240) in Bavaria if one is caught doing that. I asked if there were other fines, and he mentioned a fine of 300 deutschmarks for giving a certain other obscene gesture. The questions are: (1) Do these fines reduce the number of gestures given (do people move up the **demand curve** as the price rises)? (2) To what extent are different gestures **substitutes** whose consumption depends on the relative prices (the fines)? (3) More generally, what is the **price elasticity of demand** for giving obscene gestures?

> *Q: How elastic do you think your own behavior would be in response to a difference in fines for different gestures? If the chance that you might be caught increases, what happens to your price elasticity of demand for giving obscene gestures?*

5.6

An advertisement for a marketing consulting firm that offers seminars to businesses stated, "After you attend our seminars, your competitors will say that people would be fools to buy from anyone else, regardless of what prices you charge them." It is very hard to believe that all those **demand curves** are perfectly inelastic!

Q: If you believe this advertisement and run a business, what price will you charge your customers? Find another advertisement in today's newspaper, in a news magazine, or on television where a similarly ridiculous claim about the shape of the demand curve is implied.

5.7

At my wife's office Christmas party she "won" a set of book-plates, adhesive-backed paper that says "Ex Libris [from the library]" and on which you print your name below. These can be put on the inside covers of books you own. They are quite uncommon now but were very common until the 1960s. Why are they increasingly rare? They presumably indicate your owner-ship of something that others might borrow. Today, however, there is much less book borrowing than there used to be. First, with higher incomes, people buy books rather than borrow them. Books are *not* **inferior goods.** Second, paperbacks are now every-where, and they were quite uncommon until the 1930s or 1940s. With the growth of the paperback market, there is much less interest in borrowing someone else's hardback copy.

Q: For the same tastes—same age and education—do people with higher incomes buy more or fewer books? If more, are books a necessity or a luxury?

5.8

December 21, 2001—Media reports were that Gucci profits were down 50 percent this quarter compared to last year. In a recession the first thing people cut back spending for is **luxury** items such as Gucci products. It is not surprising that their sales, and thus their profits, are down. I would be happy to bet that grocery chains have seen much smaller declines in profits. Food bought at grocery stores has a low **income elasticity of demand,** so spending on it is relatively insensitive to the state of the economy.

Q: List three companies that, like Gucci, would experience unusually large declines in profits during a recession because the *demand for their products is **income-elastic**. List three others whose profits are likely to be pretty much immune from the recession because the demand is **income-inelastic**. Can you list any goods that would be helped by a recession?*

5.9

CBS Sunday had a feature on a couple who are deaf and whose children are also deaf. What the couple commented on, and what was apparent from the documentary that followed the family around, is how much more integrated the children are into hearing society than their parents are. The story noted that 60 percent of deaf children today have people in school whose job it is to assist them by signing for them. Partly this may be a smart move for society: The benefits in terms of the eventual productivity of the children because they learn more and can function more productively as adults may exceed today's costs. Even if they do not, however, we generally observe that wealthier societies do a better job of taking care of the less fortunate than do poorer societies. Even though caring costs more in a wealthy society because caregivers' time is more valuable, we do more of it. Caring is a **superior good:** We buy more of it as we become better off.

> *Q: Admittedly, caring is a superior good: As incomes rise, people's spending on caring rises. But is caring a **luxury**? Does the amount societies spend on caring activities rise more or less than in proportion to their real incomes?*

5.10

Problem at the Coffee Shop. My favorite local coffee shop, located three doors down a side street near an intersection with a major road, faces its most severe challenge: Starbucks has set up shop on the corner. My shop sells better-tasting coffee than Starbucks, and it charges a lower price. Nonetheless, I fear it will be driven out of business. Having observed the shop's clientele for years, I have noticed that most are regulars. I have become friendly with the owner, and I suggest to him that he should raise his price. He will still be offering his coffee at a lower price than Starbucks. My guess is that his clients have a fairly **inelastic demand,** since they come both for the quality of the product and for the ambience. Also, they are in the habit of coming. Raising prices is unlikely to drive away many customers, and it will raise **revenue** and help the shop stay in business.

> *Q: If there is lots of mobility in the neighborhood—many old residents move out, and many new ones move in—what happens to the **price elasticity of demand** facing the shop owner?*

5.11

February 8, 2002—American Airlines is getting rid of the AT&T phones on the seat backs of its airplanes (the only phones you are allowed to use in flight). American claims the reason is that demand is low because so many people have cell phones, implicitly saying that cell phones have shifted the **demand curve** for the in-flight phones. Yet you can't use cell phones in flight, so there is no competition from them in the air. A much better explanation is that the price of an in-flight phone call is too high (typically $2 to pick up the phone and $2 per minute thereafter). The **price elasticity of demand** at those prices is now sufficiently high that the **revenue** is very low. Instead of removing the phones, perhaps the airline might try cutting prices.

> *Q: American and other airlines installed the phones before cell phones became commonplace. Do you think the **price elasticity of demand** in those earlier days was higher or lower than it is now? Why?*

5.12

On its website, the university makes available the distribution of the course grades each professor gives out. One of my clever young colleagues knows this and says that he likes to give out a lot of As and a lot of Fs. This gives the students whom he wants to take his course an incentive to do so while discouraging the students he doesn't want. Students who might normally be B students think they can get an A and sign up. Students who are C or D students believe that they have a much higher than usual chance of getting an F and stay away from his courses. His grade distribution thus allows students voluntarily to sort themselves in a way that maximizes the quality of the students taking his class.

Q: Ask yourself and your friends: Would you respond to this information the way my colleague believes students do?

5.13

February 19, 2002—Last year the Texas legislature passed a law allowing auto insurers to set prices on the basis of the mileage actually driven. This seems like a good idea. Hamburgers are priced on a per-unit basis; why not price compensation for the risk of accident the same way? If that were done, people who drive relatively little would no longer be **subsidizing** the ones who drive 50,000 miles a year. Unfortunately, no insurer has yet chosen to offer this kind of pricing. I'm not surprised: How can insurers determine the mileage actually driven by each particular insured driver? Unless everyone is completely honest, cheating drivers will guarantee that insurers will lose money on this basis. The end result will be no insurance offered—or a return to the pricing scheme we now have.

Q: How would the outcome in this market differ if the insurance companies could monitor your driving electronically? Would that solve all the problems?

5.14

February 27, 2002—One of the textbooks I assign will have a new edition this July 2002 with a copyright date of 2003. It used to be that a book used the next year's copyright date only if it appeared after September 1 of the current year. That restriction seems to have broken down. So why not publish the book in January 2002 with a 2003 copyright? That way people will think it is current long after it comes out, and it might sell for longer. In textbook publishing the answer is clear: The publishers don't want the books to last too long because the used book market eats away at sales. Getting a little bit of advantage by labeling a book published in July 2002 as copyrighted in 2003 gives an extra profit. Any further "jumping the gun" confers no great advantage. In other areas, however, such as college football bowl bids and job offers, there are big incentives for people to start making deals ahead of previously agreed deadlines. Eventually some of those deadlines break down as a few buyers and sellers realize that it is to their advantage to agree on a deal ahead of the deadline. This breakdown has happened several times in college football bowl bids, although as of today colleges are adhering closely to the deadlines of the Bowl Championship Series (BCS).

> *Q: If you are the manager of the Fruit Bowl, a new bowl game, and have lots of money to bid for bowl participants, would you wait for the BCS picks to be determined? How early would you begin offering bowl berths?*

5.15

One of the perks of being a faculty member is paid travel for professional activities, usually to appear on the program at a scholarly meeting or convention. In my first year as department chair I was deluged with requests by my colleagues that the university fund such travel. It was very hard for me to say no, and at the end of the year I noticed that spending for faculty travel was more than twice what had been budgeted. One colleague had taken seven paid trips during the year. I didn't know what to do: I didn't want to spend my time deciding which proposed trips were meritorious and which were not, and I didn't want to have to say no to my colleagues. One new faculty member solved the problem. He said, "Just tell each faculty member: You have a certain amount—a lump sum [it turned out to be $750]—for professional travel. Spend it any way you want so long as it is a justifiable professional trip." This solved the problem completely: no more complaining and no more budget overruns. Each professor knew what his or her budget was when the year started and was able to choose the best possible trip or combination of trips. The young colleague had reminded me that it's always better to have a lump sum to spend than to be required to spend the same sum on a specified set of activities that you can't choose freely.

> *Q: Think back to when you were at home. Is my problem in this vignette in any way different from your parents' choice of whether*

*to give you a fixed weekly allowance or to spend the same amount
of money on specific things for you?*

5.16

Windfall—but What to Do with It? Because I flew a lot last year
my airline sent me eight coupons, each good for an upgrade from
coach to business class (to first class on domestic flights) on any
one-way itinerary in its worldwide system. It makes sense to use
these coupons on the longest flights, not to waste them on short
domestic hops. The problem is that they're good for only one
year and I have only two trips to Europe and one to Asia planned
in that time. I can use six coupons for those trips, but that leaves
two others. I could save the two coupons and use them if another
transoceanic trip arose, or I could use them on a domestic trip,
perhaps Texas to the East Coast. The latter choice seems like a
waste, but it's less of a waste than not using them at all. To an
economist the *cost-benefit* choice is (1) value of coupons on a
long trip times the probability that I will make a long trip versus
(2) value of coupons on a short trip that I will certainly take.
Right now I think there's a decent chance that another transoceanic trip will arise some time in the next year, so I'll hold on
to the coupons. Come next fall, though, with time running out
and still no other long trips, I'll probably and regretfully (since I
didn't get another transoceanic trip) use the coupons to upgrade
a domestic trip.

> *Q: If you were in my shoes and thought that the chance of
> another transoceanic trip was 50 percent, would you wait or use
> the coupons now? What if you thought that the chance was only
> 10 percent?*

5.17

March 10, 2002—In his new autobiography, basketball coach Bob
Knight (Indiana and recently Texas Tech) challenges U.S. universities to clean up their athletic programs. He repeats a proposal
he made many years ago that athletic scholarships, which are
limited in number by NCAA rules, should be reissued only if the
previous scholarship recipient has graduated. He argues that this
plan would give coaches and universities an incentive to improve

the currently pathetic graduation rates of athletes in major sports (with basketball and football being the worst offenders). No doubt Knight is correct: This incentive would improve graduation rates. It also would generate tremendous incentives for universities to skirt the restriction by creating courses that athletes could pass without taking time away from practice and games. There would also be enhanced pressures on professors by university athletic officials to give athletes grades they did not earn. Without these changes, some students who are in college mainly to play sports will not attend. With a less able pool of players, the quality of college sports will deteriorate.

> *Q: Draw a supply-demand system for college athletes at a university, with scholarship amount and availability being the "price." Show what Knight's plan would do in this "market."*

5.18

An excellent example of product demand is for auto vanity license plates. Noneconomists might imagine that there's no economic decision making in choosing whether to buy a vanity plate—vanity is vanity, and why should price matter? But the plates seem to be a completely standard good. The study estimated a **price elasticity of demand** of −1.30 and an **income elasticity of demand** of +.57. What was especially neat about the results is that demand is higher if the state government spends more tax revenue promoting the sale of vanity plates and if the program has existed longer. Quality seems to matter too: The more characters allowed on a vanity plate, the greater the sales.

> *Q: As with every good, the price elasticity of demand need not be constant across income classes. Do you think the demand is more or less elastic among higher-income families?*

5.19

The dean of our liberal arts college wants to get more of the 500 faculty members to submit proposals to foundations and governments to obtain funding for their research. If you submit a proposal, he will give you a grant of $2,000 to be used for academic travel, book purchases, computers, and the like. This incentive is designed to get faculty members to do things they otherwise would not do; it raises the returns to submitting a grant proposal. The dean's idea has two problems. The obvious one is how to police the proposals: What's to prevent me from submitting a slipshod proposal that has no chance of outside funding so that I can get the dean's $2,000? The bigger problem—one that is inherent in any **subsidy**—is how he can avoid subsidizing proposals that would have been written anyway. How can he subsidize only the marginal proposals and avoid giving the $2,000 grants to faculty members who already had planned to seek funding? He can't; his only hope is that the **elasticity of supply** of proposals is sufficiently high that very many faculty members who had been just below the margin where they would apply for grants are induced to write proposals.

> *Q: Draw a **supply curve** of proposals where the dean's subsidy will create a lot of new proposals. Draw one where his subsidy will not have much effect.*

5.20

What cell phone plan to get? The issue is the unrestricted minutes, usable at any time. They are offered on a two-part price system: You pay a fixed amount for a maximum number of minutes and then pay per minute for any time above that. The price of an extra minute is zero up to the limit; thereafter it becomes quite high. (One company offers 250 anytime minutes for a fixed fee of $30, offers 350 minutes for a fixed fee of $40, and charges 35 cents a minute if you exceed your limit.) Having bought a particular plan, you have a tremendous incentive to use all your minutes. You also have an incentive to be very careful as you near the maximum, since the cost of exceeding it is high. If you're repeatedly using more than your maximum, you have bought a plan that doesn't have enough minutes: You can do better with more guaranteed minutes. Indeed, you should buy a plan that you are nearly certain you will never exceed. That way there is no need to incur the **opportunity cost** of monitoring how many minutes remain.

> *Q: This kind of pricing scheme seems unusual. What would the incentives be if the cell phone companies simply priced on a*

per-minute basis, with no fixed charge but a higher price for any-time than for weekend minutes? Would you spend more or less on your cell phone service?

5.21

March 26, 2002—The French presidential election is coming up soon. But some people won't be able to vote—they've died in traffic accidents in the past twelve months in anticipation of the election. Traditionally a newly elected French president pardons all traffic violators upon taking office. This results in French drivers, never the most careful in Europe, taking even less care in the last year of the seven-year election cycle. This year traffic tickets are up and so are fatalities, as drivers know that the monetary penalty from traffic tickets will be wiped clean by the newly elected president.

> *Q: Surely the loss from dying in a traffic accident is much, much greater than the cost of a traffic fine. So why does waiving fines make people take this kind of risk?*

5.22

April 16, 2002—My university will be charging a flat fee to students in place of tuition per credit hour and other fees. Starting in fall 2002, any liberal arts or natural sciences student who takes twelve or more semester hours will pay $2,500 per semester no matter how many hours he or she is registered for (up through eighteen semester hours). Those taking fewer than twelve hours will still pay on a per-credit basis, although the price per credit is higher than that for full-time students. This change was stimulated by concern that the typical student takes around five years to graduate. With the flat fee the price of an extra credit hour beyond twelve is zero. Students will have an incentive to take as many credit hours as quickly as they can. While its revenues per student may not rise and may even fall, the university hopes that the change will increase its "product," the number of students graduating each year.

> *Q: Given the new incentives, why wouldn't students take twenty or twenty-five credit hours per semester and graduate in three years?*

5.23

My mother-in-law telephones my wife long distance, Boston to Austin, at least once and occasionally as many as three times a day, often at inconvenient times. My mother-in-law is moving to Austin in two weeks. In Boston the calls cost her seven cents a minute. Now they will be local calls, with no extra charge assessed no matter how often she calls. With a price per extra call equaling zero, will she call us even more? What is her **price elasticity of demand** for these calls? I hope her demand is inelastic; otherwise my poor wife will be deluged with calls. If the price elasticity of demand is much different from zero, the only hope is that her **demand curve** might also shift leftward. With my mother-in-law being in Austin, my wife can visit her more in person, and perhaps personal visits and phone calls are **substitutes**.

> *Q: Is your demand for long-distance calls fairly* price-inelastic *or* price-elastic? *If you own a cell phone, how has that affected your price elasticity of demand?*

5.24

A senior scheduled to graduate this term was failing a course. He decided to download a term paper and turn it in as his own work. Since his prior record is clean, the university's most severe punishment for cheating in this case is for him to fail the course. The student clearly optimized in light of the **incentives** he faces. Had he cheated and not been caught, he would have passed the course and graduated. Had he not cheated, his complete lack of knowledge of the course's material meant that he would surely have failed and not graduated. Cheating and getting caught leave him no worse off than he would be if he hadn't cheated at all (ignoring any moral qualms he should have had), and he at least had a chance of getting away with it and graduating.

> *Q: What could the university do to alter the incentives facing graduating seniors to make the less moral ones behave better?*

5.25

Between 1990 and 2000 the rate of workplace injuries in the United States fell 25 percent. Workplace fatalities fell even more.

These changes accelerated a trend toward safer workplaces that had been observed for many years. Are these changes the result of increased government concern about worker safety? Maybe, but the trend is also consistent with the fact that safety in the workplace is a **superior good:** As people's incomes rise, they are willing to forgo some extra earnings in order to obtain more safety on the job. It is not clear whether job safety is a **luxury** or a **necessity**; but it is certainly not an **inferior good:** The **income elasticity of demand** for safety is positive.

> *Q: What does this vignette suggest has happened to the rate of deaths from auto accidents since 1950? Check on the Web to see whether your inference is correct.*

CHAPTER 6

The Consumer— Satisfaction and Preferences

6.1

The two grandchildren and I went to a museum today. At the entrance was a sign suggesting a donation of $5 for adults and $3 for each kid, so I threw $11 in an unwatched/unsupervised container. Do most people do this? If so, why? This kind of charity must raise my **utility** (otherwise I wouldn't have done it), but why? Is reducing our guilt something that we consider in deciding what to purchase?

> *Q: Give three examples in your daily life where you have paid for things that suggested a payment but did not require one. How much did you pay, and was it as much as the suggested amount?*

6.2

October 11, 2001—President Bush exhorts us to go out and buy enough goods and services to stimulate the economy. Will we do that? Possibly, but in the end it is each person's choice: We are choosing to maximize our own happiness, given prices and given our incomes and tastes. My guess is that the President's exhortations won't have much effect. If he's really concerned about this, he might be more successful if he urged business to cut prices in the recession more than they have.

> *Q: When faced with a choice—save $1,000 to afford a spring break in Cancun or spend $1,000 now to stimulate the economy— what will you do? What if it was an extra $10 to have three more*

beers in Cancun next spring versus $10 spent now to help Mr. Bush stimulate the economy? Is your answer any different?

6.3

Utility is funny. I lived perfectly well for years without a cell phone and without a cable modem (using land phones and a dial-up connection), and right after I got them, I did not feel all that much happier. At this point, though, if they were taken away, I'd feel much worse. There's an asymmetry or ratcheting effect on happiness, at least in the short run, which keeps raising our so-called needs for goods once we have gotten used to them. Our utility depends not only on what we are currently consuming but also on what we are accustomed to consuming.

> *Q: What new goods that you have can't you live without? If one of them were taken away, would you feel worse? Would you continue to feel worse for years, or would your negative feelings diminish?*

6.4

I have only sons. Today, for the first time in my life, I had a chance to braid a little girl's (my older granddaughter's) hair into a ponytail. This was extremely enjoyable and satisfying (even though I did such a bad job that the ponytail fell apart fifteen minutes later). **Diminishing marginal utility** is real; this may even be more fun than I have had playing with my grandsons.

> *Q: How do you think I will feel about braiding this granddaughter's or my other granddaughter's hair after a few more years? How do you feel when you baby-sit and the kid asks you to read a book you haven't seen before? How do you feel when he or she asks you to read it for the tenth time?*

6.5

Would winning the lottery increase people's **utility**? A study presented at a session of research papers at the meeting of the American Economic Association studied British lottery winners.

The author found that in response to winning even a small amount in the lottery people said they were much happier with their lives. The problem is that all the other evidence suggests that Americans today are no happier than people were forty years ago, when real incomes were much lower. Apparently, overall happiness is based in the long run on what we expect. Surprises like winning the lottery and having the home team win a ball game make us temporarily happier, but that happiness dissipates after a while.

> *Q: You get an A on your next economics midterm, but you were expecting a B. How do you feel about your economics class when you get the test back? How do you feel about the class three days later?*

6.6

At a restaurant last night the menu had an eight-ounce filet mignon for $21 and a twelve-ounce filet mignon for $26. I ordered the eight-ounce filet, while a colleague ordered the twelve-ounce version. I expressed surprise and doubt that he would really want to eat that much meat. He responded, "I am not sure that I want to eat the extra four ounces, but at least I now have the option of doing so, and at the very low marginal price of $5 to get 50 percent more steak." If an extra bit of something is cheap enough, even if we think its **marginal utility** is very low, it is rational to purchase it just for the option of having it available to consume it in the future.

> *Q: Assume you would have done the same thing as my colleague. Would you still do it if the price of the twelve-ounce filet had been $28? If you would not have mimicked my colleague when the price was $26, how low would the price of the twelve-ounce steak have to drop before you bought it instead of the eight-ounce steak for $21?*

6.7

My weight is now the highest it has ever been, and I'm really unhappy about it. I have to lose ten pounds to get where I want

to be. If I could just cut out one dessert per day and not add anything else to eat, I would get to where I need to be in two
months. The problem is that cutting back a bit—a marginal
adjustment—just won't work: I know that I would forget about
my plan and/or backslide into my old eating habits. The only
workable solution is to go cold turkey: no desserts, no eating
between meals, and especially no chocolate-chip cookies from
the local bakery. With **addiction,** eating just one cookie makes
me want another—and another. Going cold turkey is often the
only way, partly because it makes it easy to keep the commitment in mind (makes it easy to plan) and partly because the
shock may be sufficient to shift me to a new equilibrium pattern
of consumption.

> *Q: Would the answer be any different if instead of being a bit
> overweight I were addicted to heroin and were seeking to give it
> up? Marginal changes, by which I slowly decrease my dosage, or
> going cold turkey?*

6.8

Our synagogue successfully raised money to construct a new
building. The building has now been occupied for a year. It needs
no repairs, but after another ten years or so it no doubt will. We
should accumulate a contingency fund for future repairs. The
problem with such a fund, the same as with any "rainy-day"
fund, is that there's a tremendous temptation to raid the fund for
frivolous purposes. It's hard enough to impose self-control on
your own consumption but much harder to impose self-control
on a group, especially a nonprofit organization. We need to find
some mechanism that would solve this problem for us. While it
is perhaps not appropriate for a synagogue, something like the
old-fashioned Christmas clubs, where you deposited $10 a week
in a bank from January through September toward Christmas
shopping and were penalized for withdrawing the savings,
might do the trick. We need to protect our "future selves" from
frivolous spending by our "current selves."

> *Q: What is needed is what economists call a self-control mecha-
> nism. List two self-control mechanisms that you impose on your-
> self to overcome temptation.*

6.9

Several years ago an economist asked undergraduates to place values on gifts received from various people. Gifts from girl-friends or boyfriends were valued at almost $1 per $1 price of the gift, and presents from parents at somewhat less. Relative to the students' valuations, presents from grandparents had the least value per $1 the grandparents actually spent on the presents. It's possible that the source of the gift matters: A present from a girl-friend or boyfriend is valued more than the identical present from one's grandparents. An economist would say, though, that girlfriends and boyfriends know your **utility** function best, while grandparents are almost clueless about what does or does not make you happier.

> *Q: If you had been one of the student participants in the study discussed here, how would you value a typical present costing $100 from your parents, your aunt Sadie, your boyfriend or girl-friend, your grandmother?*

6.10

My wife suggests that on our next trip abroad we should buy some very nice artwork for ourselves. I asked her what's going to happen to the art when we die. She said, quite correctly, that our sons would rather have our money than the objects we buy. That's always true: They can always use the money to buy the objects they might have inherited, and the odds are high that those are not the objects they would want now if they had the choice. My wife pointed out one way in which they are better off if we bequeath them the art objects instead of money: If they currently lack information on the nature of the art objects available in the world, it is possible that when they receive their bequest of art, their preferences will blossom and they will become happier than they otherwise would have been. This is *not* a paternalistic view but instead accounts for the possibility that education and/or information might enhance our sons' preferences by showing them a whole new world.

> *Q: Are there cases in which you believe your tastes have been expanded, and your subsequent behavior has changed, because*

you have been forced to consume something that you otherwise would not have consumed?

6.11

My four-year-old grandson is nuts about airplanes. That's nearly all he talks about, and he can proudly identify the logos of the major U.S. air carriers. He never gets tired of airplanes and watches the video *There Goes an Airplane* over and over. His current desire is for a model of a Southwest Airlines plane that has Shamu the killer whale painted on it. He has a very strange **utility** function: All that apparently affects his satisfaction is airplanes, and his **marginal utility** from additional exposure to airplanes in no way seems to diminish, contrary to everything we teach in economics. Are little kids not economic people? Or maybe I'm missing something in describing his satisfaction and focusing only on the one thing I hear a lot about. Maybe other things matter to him too, such as apple juice and his violin. If they do, then like every other consumer he has to worry about substituting between these activities, and the notion of **diminishing marginal utility** comes into play for him too.

Q: If you have a little brother or sister or cousin, niece, or nephew, does their behavior regarding the thing they are fixated on exhibit diminishing marginal utility?

6.12

Texas and some other states are dotted with sheds selling fireworks on a seasonal basis (before New Year's Day and before July 4). Many of them offer, "Buy one, get five free." Why don't they just cut the price from, for example, $6 per item to $1 per item and sell them one at a time? Would their **revenue** be the same if they did? I assume not, or they would do that. There are several reasons why their behavior might make sense. First and most important, this gimmick lowers the price of each of the second through sixth firecrackers to zero. Since the cost of each extra firecracker is zero, you will be willing to spend more in total than you would if each were priced at the same positive amount. If the fireworks seller is clever, the total cost of the six exactly equals the sum of what you would have been willing to pay for the first plus for the second plus for the third, and so on. This is similar to pricing of ski lifts, "all you can eat" buffets, and other such deals. In all these cases the seller is hoping, by charging the equivalent of a fixed fee for purchasing the goods or services, to get the buyer to spend more. In economists' jargon, the seller is hoping to extract the entire **consumer surplus** from the buyers, to obtain **revenue** equal to the entire area under each buyer's **demand curve** for the product.

> *Q: What might lead a seller to offer "Buy one, get five free," as opposed to offering "Buy one, get ten free"?*

6.13

Suicide is an extremely depressing topic, but one can think about it like an economist. One can imagine people rationally choosing to kill themselves if they expect little **utility** over the remainder of their natural lives. Since life expectancies are lower the older you are, an economist would expect higher suicide rates among older people, and that's exactly what we see happening. Similarly, unemployment also lowers people's satisfaction, and we know that suicide rates rise in recessions. Someone who experiences a sudden drop in income is also more likely to commit suicide. Economic factors aren't the only cause of suicide— far from it—but they do matter, and we can use simple economics to be on the lookout for people who might be contemplating suicide.

> *Q: Can you use the same arguments to predict who is more likely to commit murder? Why or why not?*

6.14

My Ph.D. student is agonizing about which of several jobs to accept. He has two offers so far, School A and School B. He tells me that he unquestionably would prefer School A to School B, but he wants to wait to reject School B until he hears whether he will be getting an offer from School C, which is his top choice. Is he being rational? No! If he prefers A to B, having C as an extra choice should not affect that preference ranking. Economists and social theorists call this notion the **independence of irrelevant alternatives.** The student was very upset when I called him "irrational" (probably the worst thing you can say to an economist) and began trying to explain how his reasoning was sensible. In the end, though, he laughed and admitted that he wasn't being very rational. But he still refuses to say no to School B until he finds out about School C.

> *Q: What if School C is preferred to School B but not to School A? Would waiting on School C make more or less sense than it did in the vignette? Would it be rational?*

6.15

San Francisco has enacted an "instant runoff" rule; henceforth people will rank their preferences for candidates when they vote. If there are three candidates and none wins a majority, the top two candidates are assigned the second-place votes of those who voted for the third candidate. Will people's first-place votes be the same as they are in the usual U.S. voting method? They should be: The **independence of irrelevant alternatives** suggests that including a second-place vote should not affect your first-place vote. Even if people do exhibit this independence, the voting scheme can result in outcomes totally different from those of a system that allows the candidate with a plurality to win. In my class in fall 1992 the students voted for president by ranking Clinton, Bush, and Perot. The first-place votes were 38 percent, 28 percent, and 34 percent. That eliminated Bush, but even though Clinton had won a plurality, Perot received almost all the second-place votes. If the sentiment in my class had been national, and if we used preferential voting to aggregate individuals' tastes, we would have had President Perot from 1993 through 1997.

> *Q: In 1996 Perot was on the ballot again (with Clinton and Dole). President Clinton received only 49 percent of the vote. Would the "instant runoff" system have made a difference then? What does that tell you about the conditions when that system will give results different from those of our usual voting system?*

6.16

I just received the $2,000 referred to in a vignette in Chapter 5. The problem is that these funds must be spent on academic travel, book purchases, computers, and so forth. Worse still, they must be spent by August 31. The funds come with both a goods constraint and a time constraint. My **utility** would be higher if I could just take the funds as a nontaxable monetary gift. That way I could spend them over an extended period on exactly the goods and services that maximize my utility. This is always true: We can always be at least as well off with unrestricted money as with money whose use is restricted (since without the restrictions we could always buy the things to which the restrictions limit us). We are also at least as well off with money whose spending has no deadline as with money that must be spent soon. What should I do? I could just use up the money on things that are not too valuable to me. Better still, though, I should find a legitimate way to break the restrictions that prevent my using the money after August 31.

> *Q: Imagine yourself getting $1,000 from your rich uncle that has to be spent on clothing in the next week. What would you buy? How would you circumvent the restrictions the rich uncle imposes?*

6.17

I'm nearing the end of writing this book. My wife says I won't be able to stop and accuses me of being addicted. How can I be addicted? Don't I have **diminishing marginal utility** so that the extra pleasure from writing each additional vignette is lower than the pleasure from writing the previous one? How can people be addicted? Don't they too get less and less extra pleasure from each extra cigarette, each extra injection of heroin, and so on? It's true that **marginal utility** diminishes at each point in time: Writing the third vignette in one day is less pleasurable than writing the first, and smoking the sixtieth cigarette yields less extra pleasure than smoking the first. But the first vignette written after having accumulated **addiction** capital—having generated lots of experience writing them—may yield more satisfaction than writing the first vignette on the day this book was started. The first cigarette smoked each day after having accumulated the addiction capital from a lifetime of smoking may yield more smoking pleasure than did the first cigarette smoked when you just began smoking. Utility has to be considered in light of the habits that one has invested in over one's lifetime—or in this case, over the duration of writing this book.

Q: List two things you do that meet the definition of addiction as implied in this vignette. Are they really addictions? Have you really gotten more pleasure out of the first one consumed in a day (or in a week) as you have consumed more over your lifetime?

CHAPTER 7

Utility—Altruism and Risk

7.1

At breakfast this morning my five-year-old grandson finished his half waffle and wanted more. I had finished three-quarters of a waffle and figured that I wouldn't get that much more satisfaction out of the last quarter. But why, since I would get some satisfaction out of it, would I (a rational person) part with it? There's more to consumer behavior than narrow individual utility maximization: There are **altruism** and intergenerational concerns. I care about my grandson and am willing to sacrifice my direct satisfaction a bit in order to increase his.

> *Q: Graph my utility as a function of the amount of waffle I have eaten, as implied by this vignette. Now draw a graph showing the satisfaction I get from the two goods, waffles eaten and waffles given to my grandson. What must be true about the **marginal utility** of the last quarter waffle eaten compared with the marginal utility of the first quarter waffle given to the grandson?*

7.2

It's our wedding anniversary, and I was thinking about the most important things we have produced: our sons (and indirectly our grandchildren). We have decided to promise them each a sum of money as a gift every year for the next eight years. We think about this as follows: The **marginal utility** to us of these extra dollars of our own consumption must be less than the marginal utility to us of the sons' families' marginal spending from this money. How far does this intergenerational **altruism** go, and why? We certainly wouldn't give anywhere near this kind of money to our nieces or nephews even though one niece could use it a lot.

> *Q: Would we give as much money if our grandchildren were adopted? Would our behavior differ if we were seventy-three years old instead of fifty-eight years old? Would we give more or less?*

7.3

October 15, 2001—What is the proper amount of caution to use in dealing with the anthrax threat? If there were no uncertainty about how widespread the disease might become, the resources to be devoted to it would be very small because it's not contagious and is very hard to spread by direct methods. With this uncertainty we should be more careful, but even here the risks don't seem very great. And remember, spending $1.5 billion to stock up on a targeted antibiotic means that resources that otherwise would be used for potentially more desirable goals are no longer available. An economist would say: Spend so that the marginal benefit of the extra spending on each loss (disease) times the chance of it happening is the same for all the losses we are trying to prevent.

> *Q: How might your attitude toward whether you personally want to spend money on reducing the risk from anthrax or another rare disease vary over your lifetime? How might your attitudes toward this kind of risk differ if you were married or if you had children?*

7.4

A study presented at the American Economic Association meeting asked whether states that pass laws requiring juveniles to wear bicycle helmets have lower rates of fatality from bicycle accidents than do other states. The answer would seem an obvious yes, but further consideration suggests that the answer is not so obvious. What if kids who have the protection of the required helmets feel safer and bike more recklessly? This change toward more risky behavior induced by the law could raise cycling fatalities as the gain from wearing helmets in accidents at a fixed speed is more than offset by more dangerous riding. In fact, however, the study's pretty careful statistical analysis shows that adopting such a law lowers fatalities by about 20 percent.

> *Q: What will happen to the average quality of the helmets that bicycle helmet manufacturers are producing if helmet laws are passed?*

7.5

Defibrillators (machines designed to restore heart rhythm during a heart attack) are dropping in price so rapidly that they will soon be affordable by individuals for home use. Some doctors applaud this development. Others are concerned that people, knowing that the defibrillators provide some protection, will reduce their efforts to stay healthy and engage in more risky behavior. Of course that's true: Whenever you are provided insurance, you take more risks. The question is, What will be the net effect? On this general issue there is a lot of guidance. For example, one study examined the impact of sex education. It showed that it does increase the amount of teenage sexual activity but does not affect the rate of teen pregnancy. A similar thing probably will happen with home defibrillators: People will take a little bit less care, but the net effect will be that heart attack deaths at home decline.

> *Q: Can you infer from this example what the likely effect of laws requiring the use of seat belts might be on driving speeds and deaths in automobile accidents?*

7.6

There's an old saying, "A bird in the hand is worth two in the bush." This is a fairly profound statement about risk and people's attitudes toward risk. If people don't care about risk at all, the saying that the utility from one bird in the hand equals the utility from two birds in the bush must mean that the chance of catching a bird is .5 (50 percent), since the expected catch is one bird. But if people don't like risk (are **risk-averse**), the chance of catching a bird has to be higher than .5: The only way that one in the hand equals two in the bush, if you don't like risk, can be if the expected number of birds caught is more than one bird. We think that most people are risk-averse. The best evidence for this assumption is that risky investments must yield higher returns if they are to attract investors. This old proverb must be implying that the chance of catching a bird in the bush is greater than 50 percent. How much greater depends on how much you dislike risk, how risk-averse you are.

> *Q: Most of us do not catch birds. But there are other activities where we can get all or nothing or something in between, say, an A or a C in a course, as opposed to a B. Which would you rather have, a 50 percent chance at an A and a 50 percent chance at a C or the certainty of getting a B?*

7.7

January 18, 2002—Today is the day the federal government was supposed to require that airlines screen all bags on all flight segments. Because this would have caused huge delays in air travel, the new requirement is that only some of the bags must be screened. This means that the government is allowing an increased risk that someone could blow up a plane on which he or she is not even flying. The government has chosen to **trade off** passengers' security in favor of saving their time. An economic calculation probably would show that that the value of the time saved far exceeds the narrow economic value of lives potentially lost to the minute risk of this type of bombing, which has not occurred in the United States in at least ten years. The question, however, is not just a simple monetary calculation but how **risk-averse** we are to this very, very small risk. If we are sufficiently concerned—sufficiently risk-averse—the federal delay is the wrong choice.

> *Q: How might the response to this issue be different in a much poorer society where people's time is less valuable? How would it be different in a country where people's life expectancy at birth is only forty years instead of seventy-seven as it is in the United States?*

7.8

March 7, 2002—I had a long-planned spring break trip to Israel to spend four days doing research with a coauthor and two days touring with my wife. The benefits of this trip are obvious: a fun vacation and a chance to get some interesting research accomplished. The only monetary cost if I don't make the trip is the $150 cancellation fee on the air ticket. But the potential cost of going is much larger and was looming larger with each additional Palestinian suicide bombing. The potential cost includes the loss from death or injury in such an attack times the risk of my becoming a victim. The risk is tiny, but the value to me of my life is huge. Figure it this way: Assume that I value my life at $10 million, about what economic experts use in their calculations. As long as the extra risk of death while there compared to staying at home is greater than $10 million/$150, in other words 1 chance in 66,667, it pays to cancel the trip. I'm uncertain what the extra risk is, but my **risk aversion** and concerns expressed by many family members made us decide to cancel out.

> *Q: How should my decision have been affected if I value my life at $1 million? At $20 million? How would you analyze the issue if I refused to place a value on my life?*

7.9

A large chain store is offering shoppers an unusual price break: If you make a large enough purchase, you can take a card from a deck. You then scratch off the covering, just as with a lottery scratch ticket, and uncover a picture showing that you have won a discount. Some cards show a 10 percent discount, some 20 percent, and some 30 percent. Why doesn't the store offer the same discount to everyone, say, 20 percent off? If people were always **risk-averse,** that would be a smart move. They aren't: A visit to the local racetrack or to Las Vegas demonstrates that. The store is offering shoppers an opportunity to gamble while they shop. Within a certain range of outcomes (most people wouldn't take bad gambles on their lives or with their life savings), people like the risks that gambling offers them. The store hopes to attract customers by taking advantage of that preference.

> *Q: Ask yourself: In this situation would you prefer a store where you knew that half the cards had a 10 percent discount and half had a 30 percent discount or one where a third of the cards had 10 percent, a third had 20 percent, and a third had 30 percent?*

7.10

Do students like risk or, like most other people, are they **risk-averse**? I'm not sure. Judging by the student who persisted in walking in the middle of the road on campus today, oblivious to the risk of death and injury from the cars trying to avoid him, they seem to like taking risks. Yet when they aren't daydreaming students are probably as risk-averse as the average citizen. The best evidence comes during class registration. We list lots of sections of introductory economics, some with instructors' names shown and others without a name. The students say that for the same class time they will invariably pick the section with the instructor's name listed. This is true even if it is not one of our better teachers. The reason is that they'd rather have someone who is just "OK" than take a chance that they might be in a section with a dreadful teacher who is assigned to the "no-name" sections. They don't seem to want to gamble that the unlisted instructor might be very good.

> *Q: You face a choice between a section of a course with no instructor's name listed and another one of the same size, at the same time, but with an instructor who you believe is an average teacher. Which section would you register for?*

7.11

It is Administrative-Professional Appreciation Day (formerly Secretaries' Day). Each of thirty-two staff people in a local office received a check for $25 from the management. Each name also was entered into a raffle to win one of eight $100 bills. People generally like lotteries; they'll gamble a small amount for a chance to win big even though on average they lose money on the deal. For small gambles they behave as if they loved risk. In this case, though, the office manager received loud complaints about the gamble, with one senior secretary saying: "I'd rather that each person received $50 [the same cost to the law firm]." Is the office staff unusual in that these people seemed to be **risk-averse** and to prefer safety to a gamble that cost them nothing and gave a few people a big return? Or is something else going on? Perhaps the staff's attitudes also involved feelings of envy and concerns about fairness; perhaps they didn't think it fair that a few might receive a lot while the rest received nothing.

Q: How do you think the staff's attitudes would differ if each staff member had been required to put up $25 for a one-fourth chance of winning $100?

Tips on Hunting for Economics Everywhere in Part I

1. Look at your own behavior and your friends' and family's behavior when you buy things or undertake a new activity. How does scarcity lead to that behavior?
2. Consider what is given up when another thing is chosen. What is the true opportunity cost of the choice?
3. Look at the choices society makes when the government spends tax dollars. What is being obtained, and what is it worth? What is forgone when the choice is made?
4. Look for cases where the government or another outside force restricts the ability of prices to equilibrate a market.
5. Look at how people change their behavior when the actual or implicit price of an activity or good changes. Are the responses large or small?
6. Consider how purchases change as income changes. How do these differences in purchases vary by demographic characteristics?
7. Look at your own behavior as it reflects the satisfaction you get from different activities. Is it rational in terms of your objectives? Does it reflect diminishing marginal utility?
8. What does behavior imply about attitudes toward risk? What does it show about altruism or envy?

Costs, Production, and Markets

CHAPTER 8

Cost and Production

8.1

A study examined the determinants of the grades of students in Economics I. The authors had data on each student's grade in the course, his or her SAT score, the number of hours per week spent studying economics, and the number of hours spent in class. This research viewed the student as a "factory," generating a grade in the course with inputs of ability (or at least SAT score) and time (spent in the two uses, studying and attending class). If each hour of the day is equally valuable and students are rational, the productivity of the last hour studying should be the same as the productivity of the last hour going to class. This didn't happen: The guys' last hour going to class was much more productive than was the last hour they studied. They could have improved their grades with no more work by studying a bit less and attending class a bit more. The women were the opposite. The **marginal product** of class attendance was zero for them: Their grades would have been just as high if they hadn't gone to class quite as often. A heartwarming additional finding was that while higher SAT scores did raise the grades, the effect of a low SAT score could be offset by a few extra hours of study each week.

> *Q: If completing more homework assignments also raises your economics grade, what should be your rule about the effect on your grade of an extra hour spent doing homework assignments compared with an extra hour spent studying or going to class?*

8.2

October 24, 2001—A student mentioned that the public agency commissioning the repair of the Queen Isabella Causeway to

South Padre Island, a resort area on the Gulf Coast in south Texas, is offering prospective contractors a bonus of $10,000 per day for each day they finish before December 23. Is this a good idea? The contractor has strong incentives to do the job quickly and with just enough quality to satisfy the public agency. Since the contractor has better information than the agency does, the quality is not likely to be very high; the job will be fast but shoddy.

> *Q: Suppose you are working for the government. Your boss asks you to create some incentives so that the contractor will build quickly but carefully. What do you propose?*

8.3

November 10, 2001—The U.S. House of Representatives has passed an investment tax credit giving companies credits (tax breaks) for investing in new equipment (as opposed to new buildings). The United States has had this policy before. At the conference I am attending today one of the participants mentioned an anecdote from the policy's previous incarnation. Some companies installed mobile lighting, which counts as equipment and was subsidized, rather than including lights as fixtures in the (unsubsidized) new buildings they had just constructed. Any **subsidy** that excludes some items will lead the beneficiaries to try to make unsubsidized items qualify for the subsidy.

> *Q: Assume the government wants to increase the hiring of high-school dropouts and offers McDonald's a subsidy for every dropout it employs. How would McDonald's behavior change? What would happen to its demand for high-school graduates? How about its demand for frying machines?*

8.4

One of our friends sells real estate in town. She now advertises "virtual tours" on the Web of the houses she is offering. This is not merely a gimmick to attract customers. In our house-buying episodes we spent lots of time driving with the real-estate agent to houses and then briefly going through them. Many of these were houses that the realtor thought we might like but that in fact failed to match our tastes. With the virtual tour the agent can give us a list of houses to "tour" on the Web. We can rule out ones that the agent thinks we'd like but that in fact are a poor match. This saves both of us huge amounts of time (and saves the agent gasoline, since she doesn't have to drive us around as much). The savings exceed her costs of constructing and maintaining the website. The **marginal product** of creating and maintaining this website is quite high.

> *Q: If you were the real estate agent, how would you calculate the monetary value from constructing a website that did this for you? Given this calculation, how much would you be willing to pay someone to construct the website for you?*

8.5

February 1, 2002—On the Super Bowl telecast this coming Sunday each thirty-second commercial will cost the advertiser $2 million. Is it really worth it? Does the ad really generate at least $2 million of extra **revenue** that otherwise would not have been received? We always assume that the companies are rational, so I guess they know what they are doing. Having an advertisement on the Super Bowl may be a prestige item: It may not generate $2 million of extra revenue, but perhaps the managers of the companies that advertise are willing to accept lower profits in order to satisfy some nonmonetary goals. That would not be consistent with narrow **profit maximization,** but it would describe behavior in a managerial corporation in which maximizing managers' satisfaction is a short-run objective beyond profit maximization.

> *Q: If you believe that the managers are maximizing their satisfaction in a company whose stock you own, what is their behavior doing to the value of your stock? How should you as a stockholder react?*

8.6

I was waiting in line at the local post office, where you take a number and get called by the clerk when the number comes up on a screen in the main room. In addition to two clerks in the main room there is a third clerk in a little office on the side. He can't see the screen, so whenever he finishes with a customer, he walks out, looks at the screen, and calls a number. He did this three times in the ten minutes I waited, taking about fifteen seconds each time. I figure he must do this about sixty times a day, taking a total of fifteen minutes walking back and forth. That means he spends at least fifty hours a year wasting the U.S. Postal Service's time this way. If he earns $20 per hour, he is wasting $1,000 per year. It's not his fault, but for no more than $500 the Postal Service could install an extension screen in his little office. This would enhance his productivity. The **marginal product** of this investment good surely would exceed its price.

> *Q: What if he did this only twenty times a day? Would it pay the U.S. Postal Service to install the extension screen then?*

8.7

February 14, 2002—I received a forwarded e-mail today listing twenty-two supposedly clever pickup lines by economists for Valentine's Day. One is "More of you is always better." This makes good sense in the context of production: If you love someone, more of that person should be better. The **marginal product** should always be positive. Another line on this list is "There is no **diminishing marginal productivity** with you." It's really hard to believe that there is never diminishing marginal productivity, even with one's spouse or lover. Eventually even the greatest romance can benefit from a (brief) respite, a bit of time apart.

> *Q: Economists are famous for being brutally frank. If you have a really strong relationship, and only if that is true, try explaining the economics in this vignette to the person you are involved with.*

8.8

Accountants include "goodwill" as an asset when they construct companies' balance sheets, but what does this really mean, and how should economists value it? That goodwill, or reputation matters, is clear; look at what happened to the accounting firm of Arthur Andersen after the Enron debacle. We can see the value of reputation only when something major and unexpected changes a firm's reputation and its value. Reputation is important, but its monetary value is very hard to measure. Given those difficulties, perhaps reputation is so loose a concept that it should not be counted as contributing to either accounting profits or **economic profits**.

> *Q: If goodwill were banned from balance sheets, how would the value of older established companies change relative to that of new companies that are just starting out? What would this do to their stock prices?*

8.9

There is "disintegration" in the auto industry: Manufacturers are shedding in-house suppliers and relying increasingly on outside contractors. The "make-or-buy" decision faces all businesses and even governments: Is it cheaper to manufacture an input yourself or to buy it from outside the firm? Inside manufacturing has the virtue of certainty and control over supply. Buying from the outside can help a company take advantage of the **economies of scale** that an outside producer who sells to a wide market might generate. Purchasing inputs can also allow a large company some **monopsony** power over its many small suppliers. The balance varies in different industries and at different times. There seems to be a general move away from integration these days as a result of declines in transportation costs and increased ease and speed of restocking depleted inventory.

> *Q: Two of my students are running a cookie business. They are trying to decide whether to buy premade cookie dough or make it themselves. What considerations should they take into account in making their decision?*

8.10

Improved Productivity or Better Living? I have been assaulted by e-mail today—from students, friends, and relatives, plus the usual huge amount of junk e-mail. All this has been made possible by the computer and Internet revolutions of the late 1980s and 1990s. Macroeconomists have argued for the last five years whether these revolutions have raised productivity in the United States, with no consensus. But what if they haven't, or haven't raised productivity very much? True, it means that workers'

marginal products may not have been raised by the improved technologies. But workers are also consumers, and the ease with which we can communicate with each other, download and play ever-fancier video games, and make travel reservations improves economic well-being. The computer and its associated technologies make us better off by raising both productivity (and eventually wages) and consumers' enjoyment. Businesses might pay for computers even if they don't raise workers' productivity if the computers make the workplace more fun and workers are willing to supply their labor for lower pay than they otherwise would require.

> *Q:* List three things you own or do that raise your productivity
> but also represent, at least in part, consumption.

8.11

Chicken and Chips. A newspaper story is headlined "Taiwan sacrifices animals so rain gods will help chip makers." There has been a drought near Taipei, and water is an essential input into computer chip manufacturing. (It takes more than silicon, chip-stamping machinery, and labor to make a chip.) With all other measures failing, government and industry officials sacrificed pigs, chickens, and ducks to the rain gods. This did generate a drizzle, but not nearly enough rain to reduce drought conditions. The question is: What is the **marginal product** of an additional chicken sacrificed? How many chickens should be sacrificed? Economic theory suggests that as with any other input, the sacrifice of chickens will be characterized by **diminishing marginal productivity.** Therefore, if the sacrificed chickens produced only a drizzle, sacrificing still more chickens is not going to add much rain. Presumably the authorities understood this economic principle, as they decided to give up on animal sacrifice as an input into chip production and rely instead on cloud seeding. Whether the marginal product of cloud seeding is any higher than the marginal product of another sacrificed chicken is unclear.

> *Q:* If animal sacrifice would help, and if they had not yet sacrificed any cattle, would a cattle sacrifice be more or less helpful
> than another chicken, pig, or duck sacrifice? Why or why not?

8.12

Just before class my economics major students were laughing at a conversation they overheard between the instructor of the previous class and her student. The student said, "I really need a good grade in this class 'cause my GPA has to be high for me to get into grad school." My students were laughing because the grade in that particular class could not have had much of an effect on the senior's GPA. The student (it wasn't an economics class, thank goodness) did not distinguish marginal from average. The same thing happens among my intro students at least once a year. Someone tells me that unless he or she gets a B in my class, his or her GPA will be so low that he or she will be thrown out of the university. These students also don't seem to know marginal from average. Their average is low because of their previous bad grades. The marginal grade—what they get in my class—is not going to affect their GPAs very much.

> *Q: Calculate your grade in this class so far and assume that it will be your course grade. What will happen to your GPA after this class? Compare that to this class's grade (the marginal grade).*

8.13

What Is Work? What Is Leisure? A group of distinguished economists is trying to place a value on what people produce at home. This matters. If more people go to restaurants and fewer cook at home, it looks like the country has a higher **average product** when in fact there has been no real change. It's producing more in the market, but it's producing less at home. The problem is that we can measure the value of the restaurant meal—it's what you pay for it—but measuring the value of a home-cooked gourmet meal is tougher. If the cooking is counted as work, should it be valued at your wage rate at your job? Or at what you would have to pay for a meal of similar quality in a restaurant? But if you enjoy cooking, maybe it shouldn't be counted at all; it's leisure, not work. There's no easy answer, which is probably why economists and others are still trying to figure out how to measure the value of what people produce at home.

Q: Think of two things that you do at home that you could instead purchase in the market. Do these things represent leisure, or are they work for you? How would you value them?

8.14

A colleague asked whether he should let his intermediate macroeconomics class go hear Paul Krugman, *New York Times* columnist and economics professor at Princeton, talk about the Argentinian debt crisis on campus next Tuesday during his class hour. The topic is clearly relevant for a macro class, especially because the course is currently covering international issues. This late in the semester the **marginal product** of the professor's time with the students is diminishing rapidly. They've never heard Krugman before and he is a good lecturer, so the marginal productivity of time spent with him would be quite high. The students should go to Krugman's lecture instead of to class, and the colleague should give a brief quiz about that lecture to make sure the students didn't just sleep in.

Q: Would the advice be any different if it were the second week of class? How should the advice depend on the quality of the instructor?

8.15

Weather has severely reduced the supply of natural vanilla, causing its price to quintuple. No one eats vanilla; it's an input into many foods, including, best of all, vanilla milk shakes. The huge price increase has led food manufacturers to do their best to **substitute** other inputs for vanilla in production. This includes increased purchases of very inexpensive artificial Chinese vanilla to use in place of the more expensive natural product. The rise in the price of natural vanilla has also spurred the development of genetically engineered bacteria that produce vanilla as a by-product. While the price of this new product is still high, it is falling, and if the price of natural vanilla remains high—if the supply of the natural product doesn't increase soon—vanilla users will start substituting toward the genetically engineered input too.

Q: What does the rise in the price of natural vanilla do to the demand for chocolate as an input into ice cream?

8.16

In "The Boxer" Paul Simon wrote and sang, "Still a man hears what he wants to hear and disregards the rest." In economics we call this bounded rationality: Consumers maximize utility and producers maximize profits, but it doesn't pay them to process all the information that constantly assaults them. A firm will not make every little change that would be required if it responded to each change in its costs or technology. This is not just a matter of avoiding costly adjustments of production to short-run changes. Instead, these limits arise because it doesn't pay firms to obtain and analyze all the information that might be relevant to decision making. Instead, a **profit-maximizing** firm will devote its resources to analyzing the information that the managers believe is most important to making profits. The rest will be disregarded.

> *Q: Consider the nearest McDonald's. List changes that you think would cause it to alter its methods of operation. List others that would change its costs but that it might not pay attention to.*

8.17

My wife and I bumped into each other while both trying to prepare breakfast. That's reminiscent of the saying "Too many cooks spoil the broth." Why should that be true? After all, if each cook's **marginal product** is positive, the broth has to be getting better and better as more cooks are added. Implicitly the proverb states that at some point the marginal product of an extra cook becomes negative, and if still more cooks are added, the quality of the broth gets worse and worse until it is spoiled. No **profit-maximizing** firm would ever get to this point, though: As soon as a cook's marginal product fell below what his or her wage was, the firm would stop hiring. Even when cooks are "free," as in your own kitchen, the proverb is correct in implying that no cook should ever be allowed to have a negative marginal product.

> *Q: Have you ever worked in an office or plant where total product seemed to decline when certain workers were present? Have you ever had roommates (or siblings) whose "help" on a task appeared to lower total output?*

8.18

Outside speakers are one input into the education that a university provides. My university paid $10,000 to Speaker A and $2,500 to Speaker B. Both received their market wages for giving speeches. Speaker A's audience contained 200 people, and so did Speaker B's audience. Speaker A's price per audience member was therefore $50, four times as much as the $12.50 that Speaker B cost per student. Like any firm, the university should be sure that the *ratio of marginal products of its inputs equals the ratio of their prices*. In this case, that means that the university should hope that Speaker A's benefit per student was four times that of Speaker B, since he cost four times as much per student. From what I've heard, Speaker A's **marginal product**—the value per student of the knowledge he imparted and the ideas he stimulated—was actually less than Speaker B's. The university could have done better by having Speaker B talk twice and not inviting Speaker A.

> *Q: If the University could obtain Speaker C, who charges $500 and would attract 300 students, should it hire her or hire Speaker B?*

CHAPTER 9

The Firm in the Short Run—Fixed and Variable Costs

9.1

Last night my wife made dough to bake *rugelach*, a Jewish baked delicacy sort of like cinnamon twists. This morning she announces to me that she mistakenly used whole-wheat flour and doesn't think the treats will be as good as usual. She says, "I haven't done the time-consuming work yet, so I think I'll throw out the dough and start over again tonight." This decision requires a conscious balancing of benefits and costs. The benefit of throwing out the dough is that the final product will taste somewhat better, but she will have to incur the **fixed cost** (making the dough, this time with white flour) again. The scary thought is: What if she had already rolled out and twisted the treats? Would she then have gone ahead and cooked them, knowing that they would not be as good as usual? How bad would they have had to be if she had already rolled and twisted the dough before she threw everything away and started again?

> *Q:* *Have you ever done an experiment for a biology or chemistry class where you knew you made a mistake early on and had to decide whether to continue? What did you do then? What would you have done if you had made the mistake further along in the experiment?*

9.2

September 28, 2001—The new Arnold Schwarzenegger movie, *Collateral Damage*, involving a terrorist attack, was ready for release in October. It is not being released as planned, and it may never be released (despite the producer having spent $70 million on it). The $70 million spent on the movie thus far is a sunk cost, and there are still millions to be spent in promotion and other costs. If people are so uninterested after September 11 in watching this kind of movie, the producers are correct in not wanting to throw any more money into it. Perhaps they can wait a year or two and release it when consumers are less repulsed by movies about terrorist attacks than they are now.

> *Q: In fact the movie was released in February 2002. What does the producer's decision to release it tell you about his or her perceptions of the changing demand for the movie? What does it tell you about the relationship between the extra **revenue** to be gained and the **variable** (advertising) **cost** he or she has to incur in February promoting the movie?*

9.3

September 30, 2001—If you give somebody a pile of money independent of whether that person does something in return, he or she will pocket the money, maybe say thank you, and go ahead and do whatever he or she would have done anyway. Economists say: "Sunk costs are sunk." Thus nobody should have been surprised that despite the alleged lack of passengers, all the flights to and from Boston next weekend on American Airlines have been filled; they've canceled large numbers of flights and laid off over 10,000 people. The public has given them a gift—no strings attached—of a "bailout" totaling over $500 million, and they have pocketed the money and made decisions comparing **revenue** to **variable cost**, ignoring the bailout money we gave them. For each flight they are comparing price to **marginal cost**—the change in total variable cost generated by operating that flight.

> *Q: In the late 1970s the U.S. government gave the Chrysler Corporation a similar "bailout" on the grounds that it would save many employees' jobs. What do you think happened to employment at Chrysler over the next few years?*

9.4

Universities offer summer school classes for a variety of reasons. I hope when my university offers a class in the summer that the people doing the planning are thinking economically. The university has a fixed plant that will sit idle if it is not used in the summer. The university thus shouldn't worry about the **fixed cost** of the buildings, but **variable costs** are still important. The professor's salary and fringe benefits are extra costs that wouldn't be incurred if he or she were not teaching the course. The building must be cooled (no small issue in Texas in August), and lighting must be provided. Also, the extra cost of registering the students for the summer must be paid. If the tuition payments of the students who signed up for a summer class don't cover these variable costs, the university should think carefully about whether to offer the course. If it offers the course at a tuition that doesn't even cover variable cost, the university is choosing to subsidize students to attend summer school.

> *Q: Say the professor's salary and benefits for teaching the course are $5,000, the extra electricity for air-conditioning and lighting costs $500, and the extra cost of registering the students in the class is $50. How much tuition* **revenue** *will have to be received to justify offering the course? Given what tuition charges per course are at your college or university, how many students need to sign up for the course to make it worthwhile for your school to offer it?*

9.5

In the movie *Fight Club* Edward Norton's character tells a fellow airplane passenger that he works as a "recall coordinator" for an automobile company and that the job is simple: "Multiply the size of the out-of-court settlement of a lawsuit times the number of cars times the probability of an accident. If less than [some level of cost] x, no recall." This expected value calculation is a good **profit-maximizing** strategy for a (heartless) car company if it doesn't care about risk. If it does, the policy leads to too few recalls: It ignores the chance that one big, although unlikely, lawsuit will bankrupt the company. It also ignores the possibility that enough bad publicity will lead consumers to demand fewer cars, costing the company **revenue** and reduced profits.

> *Q: Do you think that a small company would be more or less likely than a large company to be concerned about the kind of risk described here? Why or why not?*

9.6

Prices of color TVs in China are plummeting. The Chinese government essentially has guaranteed manufacturers in that country that their workers' wages will be paid no matter what the firm's **revenue** is. Workers' wages don't really cost the companies anything—the government has converted labor costs into a **fixed cost**. Firms can now cut prices and need only cover the relevant remaining costs—their **variable costs**—to still make a profit.

> *Q: If labor costs become fixed costs, what are left as variable costs? Graph the typical firm's **average fixed cost** and **average variable cost** before and after labor costs are subsidized. Then answer the question: Why would these companies lower their price to the point where their profits are negative?*

9.7

My wife's law firm has four empty offices in the building that it owns. It could hire four young lawyers whose fees might not cover the costs of the space, but in the short term, since the space is a **fixed cost** to the law firm, all the young lawyers need to do is bring in sufficient fees to cover their salaries and benefits and the marginal secretarial services they use. Unless the young lawyers are very unproductive, hiring them would seem like a good economic decision.

> *Q: What should the law firm do? Are there alternatives to hiring young lawyers that would allow the law firm to recover the fixed cost of the space?*

9.8

I run long-distance or work out in the gym, trying to avoid doing the same thing two days in a row. This morning I went to the gym at 5:30 AM, but it wasn't open yet even though it was scheduled to be open then. I stood in line for ten minutes, and it still hadn't opened. Should I wait around or go home and go for a run? Remembering lectures about the firm in the short run, I realized that **fixed cost** (the time I had already spent) shouldn't matter. I assumed that it would be awhile before the gym opened, and since I had neither run nor worked out yesterday and had only a limited time left to exercise, I left the line and went home for a run.

> *Q: How should my reaction (or yours if you were in this situation) differ if I had exercised every day for the previous three days? What if I had been unable to exercise for a week? Why the difference?*

9.9

A lot of the musical events my wife and I go to are on workdays. By the time the show starts at 8 PM we're pretty tired after a full day's work. By the intermission we say to ourselves, "Why stay for the second half? We've gotten a lot of enjoyment already, the marginal enjoyment is small, and we're exhausted." Nonetheless, most times we stay. You would think we would realize that we would view the prior purchase of the ticket as a **fixed cost** that shouldn't matter to us, yet it does. This is quite common behavior. While businesses may think only about the dollars in their marginal decisions, people have more than just dollars in their utility functions. Having already spent the money, we have a mental commitment to the entire show and will stay even though a simple marginal consideration that looks only at future costs (in this case, our increasingly valuable time) and benefits (the remainder of the show) would lead us to go home at intermission.

> *Q: Why even buy the ticket, knowing that it is likely that we will be ready to leave at intermission yet will feel we have to stay?*

9.10

One of the teaching assistants from last semester's class came by my office asking me to write a recommendation for an internship he is seeking. I said I'd be happy to do so. He then asked would it be OK if he used my name for other internships or jobs he might seek. I said, "Of course: The marginal effort required for additional recommendations is almost zero once I've written the first recommendation." He seemed a bit surprised by my reaction, but the **marginal cost** of writing more recommendations is tiny, since I have an electronic version of the letter on file. (The gain to him in terms of potential jobs is the same for each additional letter I write.)

Q: I always tell students to bring all recommendation requests to me at one time. How are the costs to me different compared with what they would be if I handled them one at a time?

9.11

A student who did very well in my principles class last semester came by to ask about other classes to take. After he received the usual advice, including an offer to steer him to the better teachers of economics, he flatteringly (and naively) asked if I teach all the courses in the curriculum. I chuckled and said no, of course not. The reason, I told him, is that teaching a course requires incurring large **fixed costs** of generating lecture materials and organizing notes. For that reason I, like professors at every college and university, try to repeat courses as much as possible. By doing that we can spread the fixed cost of generating the course over as many units of output (number of times teaching the class) as possible.

Q: Given my response, if you were a professor and had to teach four courses per semester, would you rather be in a faculty with five economics professors or one with forty economics professors? As a student, how do you think the quality of teaching differs if each professor is responsible for teaching all the courses in the curriculum, compared to a situation like the one I described in my response to the student?

9.12

A nursing home in town has more beds than it can currently fill. What they have done is use the nursing home bedrooms for assisted-living residents, senior citizens who do not need nursing care but can't live entirely on their own. The difficulty is that nursing patients pay much more than do assisted-living residents. The director of the home is upset about this and believes he is losing money on each assisted-living resident. He's right: He is losing money compared to his **average total cost,** but unless there is a list of nursing patients who would take the rooms and can pay the higher price, he should not worry about it. While he is losing money on the existing people, he is more than covering all costs except the **fixed cost** that he already incurred when the building was constructed. If he threw the assisted-living residents out and left the rooms empty, he would lose the entire fixed cost.

> *Q: List some other fixed costs besides the costs of the building that make keeping the assisted-living residents even more advantageous for him.*

9.13

The local specialized cardiac hospital is now advertising that it has reduced the price of a "Heart Saver CT (CAT scan)" from its usual $300 to only $100. It advertises, "This is a great way to make sure there are no signs of heart calcification building up which can cause heart problems later on." I am sure that they mean well and wish to prevent more serious heart disease, but economic considerations must have a lot to do with their decision to cut the price so drastically. First, the CAT scan machines are already in the hospital, are not fully utilized, and represent the majority **(fixed) cost** of the scan. The $100 is still above **marginal cost.** Second, this specialized hospital faces competition from a nearby general hospital that is trying to expand its cardiac unit. The Heart Hospital hopes to get patients and their doctors accustomed to the idea that theirs is the hospital of choice for any future cardiac problems.

> *Q: Assume that the $300 price covered the **average total cost** of giving a CT scan. What would have to be true about **average variable cost** for it to be sensible to offer the new lower price?*

9.14

Several of my statistics students complained today that they are having trouble finding a term paper topic. Finding a topic is equivalent to incurring a **fixed cost:** Until they've found a topic they have nothing. Once they have decided on a topic they are ready to incur the variable cost of finding data, thinking about the topic some more, doing the statistical work, and writing up the results into a term paper for the course. They—and any student—should think about writing assignments this way. This means that if the topic turns out to be a bad one, you should discard it before you sink more (time) costs into it. Also, spending immense amounts of time worrying about which topic to choose is irrational: By itself those costs of searching have rapidly **diminishing marginal productivity,** and until you actually start working on the project, you don't know if it will "pan out." Minimize the fixed cost of finding a topic by discarding unpromising topics. That way you don't become wedded to what turns out to be a bad idea.

> *Q: Is the answer any different if you have three terms papers in one semester? Does the existence of these fixed costs explain students' interest in using an expanded version of a term paper in two separate courses?*

9.15

The guy on the elliptical trainer next to me at 5:30 AM today asked whether I have teaching assistants (TAs) in my large micro principles class. I said yes (and thought that the production process requires my labor and TA labor—we're the human inputs into production). Between gulps for air he then asked, "How many TAs?" I am typically offered five TAs to help with the 500 students in the class. The problem is that the **marginal products** of the fourth and fifth TAs are low. They're low both because of the way I organize my grading and exams and because the marginal TAs assigned to me are typically new and inexperienced graduate students. On the cost side I don't pay any money for the TAs, but the more TAs I have, the more time and effort I must spend coordinating their activities and supervising them. Worse still, the required effort rises very rapidly as the number of TAs rises. So with declining **marginal "revenue"** and rising **marginal "cost,"** I don't want all five TAs. I just thank the department chairman and tell him that three good TAs are enough to do the job just fine.

> *Q: In many universities a "head TA" supervises an army of TAs for the professor who does the lecturing. As a student, how do you*

*feel about this? Is this a gain in the "output" of the course? Does
it result in improved learning for you, the student?*

9.16

Vignette 2.8 refers to a very long movie that was boring right
from the start and that continued to be boring. We went to that
movie on New Year's Eve, a night when we had planned to see
the movie then go out partying. After one hour we were ready to
give up on the movie and leave the theater, having wasted our
money on the $7 tickets. Being an economist, I said: "Let's wait,
it's almost over. Our tickets are a **fixed cost,** but the remaining
variable cost must be tiny, since the movie can't last more than
forty-five minutes more." After another forty-five minutes we
debated leaving and again decided that the remaining variable
cost—the time left in the movie—had to be small. This happened
two more times, resulting in our enduring three and a half hours
of boredom. We hadn't ignored the nature of fixed cost. Rather,
we kept on underestimating how large were the variable costs (of
staying longer in the theater). We weren't irrational, just badly
informed about the length of the movie.

> *Q: What if we had known how long the movie was right from
> the start and had paid $20 for the movie tickets. What should we
> have done after one hour?*

9.17

The publisher has offered me an advance—up-front money before
I finish this book. I will also make 15 percent of the net price (the
price your bookstore pays the publisher) on each copy that is sold.
The advance will be deducted from these subsequent payments.
My wife and I were talking about how I can get the publisher to
advertise more to sell more copies of the book. Without thinking, I
said that I ought to ask for a bigger advance; that way the publisher will want to recoup the advance by advertising the book
more. My wife pointed out that my statement was wrong: The
advance is a **fixed cost** to the publisher. Since it already has given
me the advance, its profits from publication are unaffected by the

size of the advance. If the publisher is clever, it will choose an advertising budget that maximizes its profits regardless of the size of the advance or any other prepublication costs it paid out.

> *Q: If I were to agree to take only 10 percent of the net price, would the publisher try to sell more books by advertising more? Write down what my agreeing to this lower payment does to the publisher's **marginal cost** and derive the publisher's **profit-maximizing** production.*

9.18

Deciding how to read this book requires an economic decision. Biological studies of learning suggest that people learn better if they spread the same total amount of time over more individual sessions. "Cramming" for exams is not as good a way to learn as is steady studying done regularly during the semester. For example, ten times the marginal gain from reading two pages of this book at one sitting exceeds the marginal gain from reading twenty pages at one sitting. So why not read the book in two-page units? Each two-page reading session requires you to decide to begin the book, drop your other activities, pick up the book, open it, and so forth. While the benefits from this approach exceed those from cramming the book, the **fixed costs** of this approach are so large that it is not a sensible economic decision. Most people will make the smart economic decision to read the book chapter by chapter, even though they'd learn more by reading just a few vignettes at a time.

> *Q: Compare this book to your math textbook. Are the fixed costs of studying this book regularly higher or lower than those for the math book? Are the gains to regular study, compared to cramming, higher or lower? What do these considerations tell you about how you should study the two given the scarcity of your time?*

9.19

A consultant lectured to my wife's law firm about when to settle a case that it is defending and when to refuse to settle with the plaintiff and push on toward a trial. He was basically talking about the economic decision facing every firm: pushing out to the point where the **marginal revenue** becomes less than the **marginal cost.** Say we're talking about whether to push a case for another month. The marginal benefit of pursuing the case is the reduction in the amount the plaintiff is willing to settle for. The marginal cost is the value of the attorney's time spent on the case in that month. When the defense attorney's costs are rising rapidly and the eventual settlement he or she foresees is dropping slowly, it pays to settle quickly. The problem this ignores is uncertainty about the settlement: The attorney has a good idea of the costs but doesn't know how much the other side is willing to settle for and doesn't know how much a judge or jury might award. Uncertainty makes the economic decision extremely difficult. But the comparison of marginal benefits and costs still should enter into the attorney's decision.

Q: What happens to the defense attorney's calculations if the state enacts a law that limits jury awards to $250,000?

9.20

This One Is for the Birds. Texas has been the home of the boom in emu ranching. In the late 1980s and early 1990s there was a speculative boom in emus, the Australian equivalent of ostriches. Prices for eggs and chicks skyrocketed as ranchers foresaw that emus might replace cattle as a cash crop. Unfortunately, while a small market for emuburgers was created, the price of a breeding pair of emus had fallen by the late 1990s from $4,500 to $20. The supply of emus was huge, and there was little demand. What is an emu rancher to do? The **variable cost** of raising an emu to slaughter weight—the cost of feeding the emu—was less than the price of a mature bird. Not surprisingly, smart farmers simply released their emus into the wilds of Texas. The local paper headlined, "Abandoned emus run amok on Texas roads," and several of the flightless birds wound up being hit by cars at night on rural roads.

Q: How high would the price of adult emus have to be to lead farmers to raise chicks to maturity?

9.21

With my wife away for nearly a week I'm discovering that maintaining a large house alone is really tough because food shopping and arranging for repairs and servicing take time. The dishwasher, washing machine, stove, and other appliances get more than half as much use and are almost as likely to need repairs if one person is using them as they do if two are. There are **economies of scale** in running a household. Two cannot live as cheaply as one, but their living costs won't be twice as high as those of a single person. These economies of scale provide a good reason for having a roommate, cohabiting, or marrying. They explain why the U.S. government takes account of the size of a household in calculating the purchasing power of families' incomes—the true standard of living.

> *Q: What if three adults, or four, live together? Does the household continue to benefit from economies of scale as more and more adults are added?*

9.22

Luke 13:6–9 recognizes **opportunity cost, fixed cost, and variable cost:** "A certain man had a fig tree . . . and said unto the dresser of his vineyard, Behold, these three years I come seeking fruit on this fig tree, and find none: cut it down; why cumbereth it the ground? And he answering said unto him, Lord, let it alone this year also, till I shall dig about it, and dung it; and if it bear fruit, well; and if not, then after that thou shalt cut it down." The dresser realizes that the fixed cost (the three barren years) that annoy the owner have gone by. He also knows that the land has a positive opportunity cost—another tree can be planted there. He believes, though, that incurring a bit more variable cost (the digging and dunging) might have a high **marginal product** (lots of figs) and that this **marginal cost** is worth paying, but only for one year. After a year he assumes that the marginal cost of another year of dunging and digging is not going to make the tree more productive, and the tree should be cut down.

> *Q: How would the dresser of the vineyard have responded if the fig tree had been barren for nine years? Why might his answer have been different even though both three years and nine years of barrenness would represent fixed cost?*

9.23

Such a Deal! I was planning to buy a nineteen-inch CRT display for my home computer, priced at $479 (with an eighteen-inch viewable area). But a local discounter is offering an 18.1-inch (all viewable) flat panel display for only $749. These usually sell for $1,200, and I've never seen one offered for less than $1,100. Why so cheap? It's a well-made monitor, manufactured originally for Gateway Computer Corp. The discounter is making some profit on this monitor, so the cost to the discounter must be less than $749. Gateway had ordered too many monitors from its supplier and chose to sell the excess to discounters. I will be the beneficiary of Gateway's choosing to absorb some of the **fixed cost** it created for itself when it bought the monitors from its suppliers. Gateway apparently has chosen to sell off the monitors rather than incur the **variable cost** of storing them until the demand for PCs picks up again.

> *Q: Gateway has been losing money recently. How would that affect its decision to sell off these excess monitors to discounters?*

9.24

April 19, 2002—No more Dr. Pepper on American Airlines. As part of an effort to cut costs since September 11, American Airlines has made the **profit-maximizing** decision to get rid of all Dr. Pepper products. Having this additional drink (and all other Dr. Pepper products) generates both **fixed costs** (ordering and inventorying the drinks) and **variable costs,** in this case the **opportunity cost** of the scarce space on the beverage cart that flight attendants push down the airplane's aisle. Customer service people at American Airlines inform me that demand for Dr. Pepper is quite low; apparently, most people think it tastes like cough medicine. Once again, someone with unusual tastes—who else but a Texan wants to drink Dr. Pepper?—must forgo a favorite product because a firm must incur fixed costs if it wants to offer the product to its customers.

> *Q: Would this problem arise if the airline didn't give away the drinks but instead sold them?*

9.25

A local bakery advertises that it is open from 9 AM to 6 PM Saturdays. But at 4:45 PM today signs on its door read "Sold out" and "Closed." Is this a sensible policy, not having enough baked goods to allow the store to remain open each day for the listed hours? Yes. The baker does not know how demand fluctuates from day to day. If she always baked enough—if she incurred the fixed cost of baking a huge amount every day—there would be leftovers on most days that would be wasted or sold at very low prices. It is better to run out once in a while than regularly to incur the costs of producing goods that will not be sold. But if she runs out on many days and at random times of the day, customers will stop coming. On most days fluctuating demand will ensure that there will be leftovers even at 6 PM.

> *Q: How would the baker's decision about how much to bake each morning change if the amount of day-to-day fluctuations in demand increased? How would the number of days on which she closed early change?*

9.26

The Wall Street Journal tells of jet-setters who are deserting South Beach (Miami, Florida) because the trendy clubs there have become less exclusive. How exclusive should a club be? Each club faces a profit-maximizing decision, just as firms do. So do professional associations that award honors to their members. If there is too little exclusivity, existing members won't feel that it is worth belonging to the club. Too many awards, and previous recipients feel their prize has been devalued. Each club or association should continue to admit people or give out awards until the marginal value to the association or club of having one more member or one more recipient of an award falls below the cost to the club in lost membership or in disgruntled prior winners of its awards.

> *Q: Apply the reasoning here to honorary societies at your high school or to a fraternity or sorority.*

9.27

After completing their course work, graduate students seeking a doctorate are admitted to candidacy. Typically, they submit a proposal for a doctoral dissertation for the approval of a committee of faculty members. At a meeting on a mediocre proposal one of the other faculty members (not an economist) said, "We have a lot invested in him; we can't let him fail." That's really not the issue; our past time and money spent on the student are **fixed costs.** The only question the faculty should consider is whether it is worth spending additional time and money on the student— whether he can produce a satisfactory doctoral dissertation. If the chances of his producing a satisfactory dissertation are very low, it is not worth spending any more time and money on him.

Q: Should the faculty's decision be affected by whether the student has spent two or four years taking classes? Why or why not?

CHAPTER 10

Competitive Markets in the Long Run

10.1

I spent a half hour today looking for a cake dessert not made with milk products, one that, consistent with Jewish dietary laws, can be eaten after a meat dinner. None seemed to be available in Austin. Why is the equilibrium quantity zero in what should be a competitive market? Perhaps there just is not enough demand for such cakes given the costs of setting up a network to provide them.

> *Q: What would be the characteristics of cities where I would be most likely to find such a cake? Are there dietary issues in your own religion, or do you have preferences for unusual products that cannot be found where you live? Why aren't they available?*

10.2

Why do cell-phone companies essentially give away minutes on weekends and nights? At those times there is much less demand, with lots of excess capacity. The **marginal cost** to the companies of handling another call is nearly zero. During weekdays the spectrum is clogged with callers. The marginal cost of handling another call is the cost of building additional facilities, which is much higher. The system of a low price for weekends and a high price for weekdays is dictated by competition, by the differences in the marginal cost of providing the service at the two different times. The only way companies will offer calling time during the week is if they can cover the cost of building. On weekends each company can make a profit just by covering **variable cost,** and if a company raised its price, others would lower theirs back to a very low **average variable cost.**

> *Q: It turns out that the cell-phone companies have apparently overbuilt: There is excess capacity in their systems. What does that tell you will happen to the price of cell-phone plans, even for minutes during prime time, over the next few years?*

10.3

We just rented a house in Stone Harbor, New Jersey, for a week next summer. Stone Harbor is a long, narrow island, with the west side on a saltwater inlet and the east side on the Atlantic Ocean, with First Avenue nearest the ocean, and Third Avenue nearest the bay. Bayfront rentals are slightly more expensive than those for houses nearer to Third Avenue, and prices stay the same until you get fairly close to First Avenue moving eastward. After that the rentals skyrocket, with the price for oceanfront rentals being three times that of rentals between Second and Third avenues. Why is the price in **competitive equilibrium** for an oceanfront rental so very much higher when one can walk to the ocean beach from Third Avenue in less than ten minutes?

> *Q: Give an answer for this question—if you can. Is it that the ocean view is so highly valued? Is it prestige? What do you think will happen to the difference in rental prices between the houses near the ocean and those farther away as the number of people wanting to spend time in Stone Harbor expands?*

10.4

An article in *The Economist* describes an amazing market. An exchange has been set up where firms trade/buy/sell unused bandwidth (available for data transmission, Internet use, etc.). If one company is not using its data-sending capacity, it puts it online for auction. This is a very nice commodity in which a market can arise, as it is easily transportable without loss of value.

This market arises because technological improvements allow the reduction of waste and a reduction in **long-run average cost.**

*Q: Draw a graph showing what you think the long-run average cost curve in this new industry looks like. Is this a market that is likely to sustain perfect competition, or are there **economies of scale** that will cause competition to break down?*

10.5

January 26, 2002—One of the depressing things about the Enron bankruptcy is what it says about the nature of competition in the United States. Much of the reason for the bankruptcy is the ability of the company's executives to hide shady but legal accounting practices from public scrutiny. Economists say that a competitive outcome requires perfect information, but if information about how well a company is doing is unavailable because the officers can legally hide it, how can competition function? How can capital markets (such as the stock market) allocate capital efficiently among competing uses if the suppliers of loanable funds can't tell which companies merit their confidence? While competition can be efficient, in an economy with huge numbers of companies and national or international capital markets, **efficiency** requires that information be clearly, immediately, and accurately supplied to investors, workers, and customers. The Enron debacle, like so many similar debacles in the 1920s that led to federal regulation of stock markets, shows that unregulated executives are unlikely to be very forthcoming with this information.

*Q: Why don't stockholders rise up and get rid of executives who engage in this kind of shady behavior, since in the end the stockholders, as in the Enron case, lose out? How does shady behavior affect the firm's **short-run average total cost** curve? Its **long-run average cost** curve?*

10.6

The economics editor of a major commercial textbook publisher mentioned a very interesting problem facing his company. They sell an increasing share of their books internationally. The profit on those books is much lower than the profit on domestic sales. Competing textbooks that are printed abroad are of much lower quality, with inferior paper and fewer colors. To compete with these books when it sells to international wholesalers, his company must charge a low price. He then mentioned a problem in a related market: The used textbook market in the United States has been growing. He and his colleagues believe this has occurred partly because international buyers buy up used copies of the low-priced textbooks that originally were sold abroad. They then ship them back to the United States, where they are resold at the high price in the U.S. market for used books. The original publisher finds the market for new books in the United States undercut but has made only very low profits from the international market. The solution, so he claimed only half jokingly, is a textbook that self-destructs after one use. Only that way can low-average-cost products be excluded from the market.

Q: If this publisher's analysis is correct and the market for new U.S. textbooks here is trimmed, what does this behavior do to the amount that publishers are willing to pay to textbook authors? What will happen to the supply of new textbooks?

10.7

January 29, 2002—My undergraduate teaching assistant from last semester, who is a Mexican citizen, came by to chat. She remarked that the fraud in Enron and the level of cheating gave her a rare feeling of uncertainty but one that she feels most of the time in Mexico. Her feeling has broader implications for economic development. One of the crucial things for an economy is that people can take risks within an overall framework of certainty. There is certainty that no illegalities or surprising government interference will prevent them from being successful and certainty that if they are successful, they can keep an expected share of the returns to that success. Without this kind of certainty—the knowledge that there are rules that reward success and punish failure—individuals and businesses refuse to take risks. Their refusal leads to less risk taking that can advance the country's economy.

Q: Find a newspaper or magazine story describing other behavior in the United States that increases the level of uncertainty and leads to less risk taking. Look for a story that specifically illustrates this problem in a developing economy.

10.8

There have been a number of stories recently about instant "dates," a "market" in which single women are seated at a long table and single men sit down for a three-minute date with a woman. At the end of the three minutes each party makes a note of whether he or she would be interested in seeing the other again. The men then move on to the next woman, and so on, so that each person meets roughly thirty new people in a single evening. Dating can be viewed as the information-gathering activity in the competitive market for spouses. It's a way that we can find out about other people and how well they match us and we match them. It is very time-consuming at a period of life when the value of time is increasing rapidly. The instant date reduces the time costs of gathering information and makes the dating market work more efficiently. It may be a bit crude, but it is hard to argue that the instant date is more crude than singles bars, and it is much more efficient.

Q: Another market uses the same idea but has eight-minute dates. What are the relative advantages and disadvantages of using the three-minute instant date market compared to the eight-minute instant date market? Which do you think is preferable?

10.9

A woman who is planning her daughter's wedding said that the members of the bridal party were buying their dresses at a local branch of a national bridal chain store. The bridesmaids are scattered all over the United States, and that way they can be sure to get matching dresses. Nationwide bridal chain stores are a natural response to a more cosmopolitan and mobile population. If the members of each bridal party lived in the same town, nationwide chains would have no advantage other than perhaps being able to obtain volume discounts from manufacturers. With people living all over the country, nationwide chains have the additional long-run cost advantage of offering a product that will be used in only one location but that is guaranteed to be identical in style no matter where it is purchased.

> *Q: Consider a different example. The Holiday Inn motel chain used to advertise, "The best surprise is no surprise," thus pointing out the sameness of its motels all over the United States. Is the success of the sameness, and the advantage it gave large motel chains, caused by the underlying demand forces characterizing the growth of nationwide bridal shops? Or is there something else that makes the large motel chains so attractive to travelers?*

10.10

One advertisement on late-night television states, "Introducing Enzyte (*Suffragium asotas*), the reliable, nonprescription supplement for natural male enhancement" [from the website]. This is a nonprescription and presumably lower-cost competitor of the prescription drug Viagra. The website for Enzyte does not argue that it does all the things Viagra does, but it claims substantial physical changes and improvements in satisfaction by men and their partners. The price, unsurprisingly, appears to be slightly below that of Viagra. So why don't all Viagra users switch to this product? The answer is probably that it is not an FDA-approved drug (because it is a natural substance). I expect, though, that it will attract a lot of customers who would rather save on the difference in price than worry about issues of safety.

> *Q: What do you think will be the income levels of the men who buy the Enzyte? Thus, what do you believe to be the **income elasticity of demand** for Enzyte?*

10.11

In 1776 Adam Smith wrote in *The Wealth of Nations*, "The division of labor is limited by the extent of the market." One implication is that the bigger the market, the more room for specialized products. The applicability of this statement to a big city such as Austin, Texas, was made clear this morning. A pickup truck had a sign advertising www.dogduty.citysearch.com and saying that it belonged to Dog Duty Inc. The company offers to scoop things up from your lawn for $9 weekly for up to two dogs. This kind of specialized service couldn't exist in a smaller town because there wouldn't be enough business to occupy the sellers of the service on a full-time basis. But in a big town the **market demand curve** is far enough to the right—and enough people are willing to pay the high price necessary to get someone to perform this fairly unpleasant task for them—that the company can survive and even prosper.

Q: Why might this company be able to offer its services at a lower price than a company that combines this service with lawn mowing or landscaping?

10.12

Oregon and New Jersey do not allow people to pump their own gasoline. Their laws essentially mandate the employment of gasoline attendants whose major or sole function is to pump gasoline. What do these laws do to **long-run average cost** in these states? I would expect that the cost of a gallon of gasoline there is higher than it is elsewhere (controlling for state gasoline and sales taxes): Evidence from all other states shows that consumers prefer using their own time, which would be wasted anyway, to pump gas rather than pay for someone else to do it for them. The growth of "pay at the pump," which eliminates any human contact, suggests that this substitution away from paid labor in getting gasoline into people's gas tanks lowers long-run average cost. The laws in these two states prevent that substitution and force consumers there to pay higher prices.

Q: Oregon is a big state, with most of its population fairly far from borders with other states. Much of New Jersey's population lives in close proximity to New York or Pennsylvania. In which of the two states are these laws more likely to affect the equilibrium amount of gasoline sold in the state?

10.13

It is very cold in Monterey, California, today, so we go into a clothing store to buy something warm. There's a real deal—only $12.99 for a PolarFleece pullover. But there's an additional sign stating that the pullover costs $1 extra for size XXL. The large size uses more material, so it must be more costly to produce. But that's true for XL pullovers compared to L pullovers, for L compared to M, and so on. Why doesn't the company charge higher prices for each larger size generally? After all, Burger King charges more for a Whopper than for a Whopper Junior. If they don't, and the bigger ones cost more to produce, it means that size M people are paying a price above **average total cost,** while big people are paying a price below average total cost. The reason must be that it is too costly for manufacturers and wholesalers to price the different sizes differently and for stores to mark and advertise separate prices on each item distinguished by size. Some distinctions can be made; for the few pieces of very large clothing it may make sense to have a separate price. Beyond that, it just isn't worth incurring the costs of listing many prices, putting more complex programs in cash registers, and so on.

Q: If manufacturers started pricing each different size differently, would retail stores start charging differently by size?

10.14

I always thought that mini-golf was a product of the 1950s, but it started in 1927 and spread like wildfire all over the United States. Entry was easy, and the profits obtained from the first courses built were enormous. What followed is standard in competitive industries. Attracted by huge potential profits, entrepreneurs built immense numbers of courses, usually quite cheaply and with little distinguishing one from another. As the growth of demand slowed and the market became saturated, most of the courses were soon losing money, and large numbers went out of business. Today the industry has stabilized, partly because the demand is more stable. Partly, too, higher entry costs have changed the business: Except for a few purists, most people today insist on waterfalls, mechanized swinging windmills, plastic gorillas, and other hazards that raise the cost of entering the market.

Q: What if someone invented an automatic scorekeeper to be installed on mini-golf courses? How would that change the market, including the size of the industry and the equilibrium price per game played?

10.15

What's an efficient size for a church or synagogue? If there were **economies of scale** throughout, with all the Baptists in a big Texas city such as Austin, we'd see just one giant Baptist church. With 10,000 Jews in Austin we'd see just one big synagogue. We don't: There are many churches in each denomination, as well as many synagogues. As the city has expanded, more and more different kinds of Baptist churches, Jewish synagogues, and other churches have been organized. It's not just that each one serves a local area. People drive a long way to the church or synagogue of their choice even when another one is closer. They like the peculiarities of a leader's ministry, the type of service, and even the particular social interactions of a congregation. With one big house of worship these choices would be lost. Statistical studies of the long-run average cost curves of churches suggest that this is true: There are economies of scale up to some size, but as the church or synagogue begins growing beyond a certain size, **diseconomies of scale** set in—it becomes less efficient.

> *Q: What would cause there eventually to be diseconomies of scale in churches and synagogues? List some of the cost and production factors that limit the growth of an individual church or synagogue.*

10.16

University fund-raising offices contract with private telemarketers to phone alumni who previously have not donated to the university. The university typically pays a fixed fee, and the company guarantees the university that a certain amount will be raised. What incentives does the company have to work more than enough to raise anything extra beyond the guaranteed amount? There are many suppliers of these services; the market is competitive, and each supplier would like to retain the contracts it now has and obtain others. If it barely raises the guaranteed amount, the company hurts its reputation and will lose existing customers or at least fail to attract new ones. What incentives does the university have to avoid giving the company only the most difficult alumni? Same thing—if the university gives the company the worst prospects, companies soon learn to insist on higher fixed fees and/or lower guarantees to the university. Competition, through the need to maintain a reputation, forces both parties to be honest and leads to fees and guarantees that are dictated by the costs of offering the service.

Q: Some universities do all their fund-raising through telemarketers. Would the fixed fee in those cases be higher or lower than it is among schools that provide telemarketers only the names of those who have not previously donated? Would the guarantee by the company be higher or lower?

10.17

Casinos operated by Indian tribes have expanded tremendously nationwide in the last twenty years, with some turning into billion-dollar businesses. More recently, profit-making casinos have expanded beyond Nevada and Atlantic City to a number of southern states. The Indian casinos are not liable to federal regulations on wages and working conditions. This gives them a competitive advantage over other casinos, since they can operate with lower labor costs and thus lower **long-run average cost.** The only way the other casinos can survive is by offering inferior payouts (retaining more of the money that is wagered) and hoping that not all their potential customers are lost to the Indian casinos.

Q: One state has both Indian and non-Indian casinos, while another has only non-Indian casinos. In which state are the non-Indian casinos more likely to survive?

CHAPTER 11

Competitive Markets— Responses to Shocks

11.1

I made some international air reservations over the Web today. In the past the airlines offered travel agents an 8 percent commission on tickets booked by an agent, with the airlines taking the commission out of the price of the ticket. These commissions are likely to decrease, as they have already begun to, since the travel agents must now compete with the automation of the Web. The problem is that the labor costs incurred by the travel agents necessitate at least some minimum commission. Travel agencies cannot cover costs with commissions much lower than the current ones. The new **competitive equilibrium** in response to this technical change—the development of a substitute, cheap method of booking tickets—is that the reduced number of people who cannot or do not wish to book their own tickets will still use travel agents, and eventually the travel agencies will start charging commissions to those clients to cover the agencies' costs. Travelers who are capable of booking fares on the Web will do so, and the actual Web fare will be lower than the cost of a ticket bought through an agency. The rise of "Web specials" on airline websites shows that this has already begun to happen.

> *Q: This vignette describes what eventually will be a new competitive equilibrium in this market. Graph the initial **long-run average cost** curve before the use of the Web to book travel. Then graph the new curve and show how the equilibrium has changed.*

11.2

October 16, 2001—Bethlehem Steel, one of the nation's oldest and largest steel companies, declared bankruptcy yesterday. I thought big companies had an advantage, and they used to have an advantage in steel production. But technological change in producing steel has reduced the **economies of scale** so that the minimum **long-run average cost**—the minimum efficient scale—now occurs at a smaller output than before. The big guys have lost their advantage, and many of them, like Bethlehem, are having trouble. The smaller, more flexible companies now can outcompete them.

Q: Graph the long-run average cost curve for the typical firm before and after the technological change. What happens to the number of firms in the steel market as a result of this change?

11.3

Travis County's (the county where Austin, Texas, is located) last dairy farmer is closing down his farm. "I'm tired of losing money," he said, citing declining milk prices, competition from large commercial dairies, and increasing property taxes due to rising land values. What are the implications of his closing for how cost curves shift and how firms enter and/or exit a competitive industry? One should view rising land values as increasing the **opportunity cost** of one of his inputs.

Q: Does the expansion of cities have a different impact on the profitability of large versus small farms? Draw a cost curve that would show how increasing property taxes due to rising land values might affect costs more in smaller firms than in larger ones and justify drawing the curve with that shape. What does this story tell you about how the location of farming will change as cities expand?

11.4

October 22, 2001—An article in this week's *Economist* talks about the "benefits" of recession in that a recession forces companies to try to reduce costs. While competition works, it works slowly, and the fear of going broke, which is more prevalent in a recession, helps competition work faster. Inefficient firms that might survive when times are good are the first ones to close when bad times hit. This is a silver lining in an otherwise dark cloud.

> *Q: This notion is called the "cleansing effect" of a recession. What are some of the characteristics of companies that are more likely to be cleansed by a recession?*

11.5

A wall-hanging flat-screen television is priced around $7,000 today at retail. How much will it cost in 2005? Increased competition will drive the price down. Also, as companies produce more of them, they should be able to take advantage of **economies of scale.** The price will drop a lot, perhaps even below $2,000, by then.

> *Q: Go back and find the price of a DVD player in a newspaper advertisement from 1998 and compare it to prices today. Do the same thing for a seventeen-inch CRT monitor in 1998 compared to today. Do these changes represent movements along **long-run average cost** curves, or do they represent technical changes that have shifted the long-run average cost curves downward?*

11.6

Downsizing in Major League Baseball—First Time Since 1899? Why? Major League Baseball is really one large business with interrelated plants (each team). In the last ten years demand by fans, both for tickets to the ballpark and for games on television, has not risen as fast as costs have. When this happens in any other business, the company cuts back production. That's just what may happen here. And, as in any other business, the plants to be closed are the least productive, the teams that bring in the least **revenue** (sell the fewest seats, have the smallest television audiences) and have been losing money for a long time.

> *Q: Draw the **long-run average cost** curves implied by this vignette. Then ask what economic forces caused Major League*

Baseball to expand from the sixteen teams that existed for most of the first half of the twentieth century. Draw the long-run average cost curves for that change in the market.

11.7

There's a big crisis in home insurance in Texas. Insurers are refusing to cover homeowners for mold damage. Recently there have been many large lawsuits on this, costing the insurers unexpected settlements. Nobody knows what the risks from the mold might be or how big the damages it causes could become. Insurance doesn't work when the insurers can't assess the risks: The market breaks down, and there is now no **competitive equilibrium** price at which insurance can be bought. Only after the level of risk is more certain can the market be reestablished.

> *Q: This is what economists call a "lemons problem": Uncertainty about quality in this case is so great that no one is willing to supply the product. If you were working for an insurer, could you even draw an **average total cost** curve for your product?*

11.8

A student mentioned her family's business, a small pet store. Her parents emigrated from Korea in the early 1980s and started this store in Houston. The business prospered for a while, but in the 1990s things started to go badly. The reason is that a Petsmart outlet opened nearby. Petsmart and one or two other pet superstore chains expanded tremendously during that period. **Economies of scale** in inventorying and purchasing have increased the efficient scale for production in the retail pet industry. This happened many years ago in the grocery business and in some other retailing, but it is recent in this industry. Her parents are the unfortunate victims of a change in technology that has changed the **competitive equilibrium**.

> *Q: Draw the **long-run average cost** curves describing this industry in the early 1980s. Then show how they changed in the 1990s.*

11.9

A student asked whether she should sell the textbook back after the exam. I don't know, but it started me thinking about the secondhand textbook market, which essentially didn't exist in the early 1960s. Why? The expansion of college enrollments has helped overcome the **fixed cost** of generating information in this kind of market. Also, with better information handling through the Web and with computers, the risks that a bookstore may buy back books that it can't later sell are reduced. This means the stores can afford to offer students reasonable prices for their books (or at least more reasonable prices than they could forty years ago).

> *Q: Draw the* **long-run average cost** *curve facing used textbook sellers in the 1960s and the 2000s. Now ask yourself what would happen to the equilibrium price and quantity in the used-book market if book publishers began printing new books on paper that has the consistency of toilet tissue.*

11.10

Of all the newer computer-related technologies, perhaps the most exciting is the flat-panel display monitor. Aside from its taking up much less desk space than a regular monitor, the picture is very crisp and clear. A fifteen-inch flat-panel monitor can be bought today for only $300, but the seventeen-inch panels are priced much higher, with even $600 being a tremendous bargain. It seems unlikely that the seventeen-inch panels cost more than twice as much to produce than the fifteen-inch panels. This price difference is very large given the small differences (in screen size and space taken up) in the products. Apparently manufacturers produced a lot of fifteen-inch displays, expecting them to be a hit with home users of personal computers (PCs). Instead, home users have gone for the seventeen-inch models in surprising numbers, leading to a **surplus** of fifteen-inch displays and a shortage of seventeen-inch displays. Manufacturers are now reacting to the surplus and have cut back on the production of fifteen-inch displays. Not surprisingly, the rebates that had recently helped make the price of fifteen-inch displays so low have been disappearing, and the net prices of fifteen-inch displays are rising. Presumably too, manufacturers are increasing the production of seventeen-inch displays, so their prices should be coming down. I think I'll wait a bit to buy a seventeen-inch display for my home PC even though it really would look good on my desk.

> *Q: The market appears to be moving toward a new **competitive equilibrium**, but how long does the move take? What would happen to prices of these two goods if businesses, faced with belt-tightening during a recession, suddenly cut back and start insisting that their workers have only fifteen-inch flat-panel displays with the new computers they buy?*

11.11

The local camera store and photo-finishing outlet has closed and has posted a sign urging customers to go to its central location instead. This is a fairly common phenomenon now, as the growth of digital cameras and high-quality color printers has reduced the demand for commercial photo finishing. Grocery stores and drugstores that have photo-finishing sections might be closing them down too. The question is what this decline in demand will do to the **competitive equilibrium** quantity of camera stores. Will they close, or will the shift help them out compared to non-specialty stores that have done photo finishing? The eventual location of the most efficient scale of operation in the photography business as a result of the digitization of photography is not clear at this point.

> *Q: How will these changes affect the **long-run average cost** curves facing firms that still do photo finishing? How will they affect the price of this service?*

11.12

Our favorite movie theater complex, which has seven theaters and is only three miles from our house, is closing next month. Its closing means that twenty-seven movie screens will have shut down in the last four years, all in a radius of five miles of our house. In the story about the closing one local movie buff complained, "Regrettably, it's all about economics." I agree, and the economics has to do with the growing importance of **economies**

of scale in the operation of movie complexes. Except for a very few art houses and specialty theaters (two in my town serve pizza and drinks while you watch a movie sitting on benches with tables in front of you), smaller complexes are shutting down.

> *Q: Draw the **long-run average cost** curves in the movie theater business before and after the changes that have generated the new equilibrium in movie theater complexes.*

11.13

February 19, 2002—Congress has issued a report claiming that 90 percent of U.S. nursing homes are "understaffed," whatever that means. There is some talk of legislation mandating minimum staffing requirements in nursing homes. Such legislation may improve services. It will certainly raise the cost of housing someone in a nursing home. Are the residents or their children willing to pay this higher cost? Either a lot of nursing homes will go out of business because the fees will not cover the higher costs that additional staffing will require, or there will be pressure on the federal government to provide additional **subsidies** for nursing home care. A mandate would represent a backdoor way to increase the share of nursing home costs that is covered by federal spending and thus eventually by tax dollars. Not surprisingly, President Bush is against mandates and wants to publicize the "understaffing" to encourage nursing homes to hire more staff. That seems unlikely to be effective unless it changes individuals' or the government's willingness to pay higher prices for nursing home care.

> *Q: Draw the cost curves in the nursing home industry before and after the mandate is imposed. Draw the **demand curve** for the industry's product and then infer what happens to output and the equilibrium price.*

11.14

The United States and Mexico are cooperating more on stopping drugs. The Arellano brothers, who headed the Tijuana drug cartel (they were the prototypes for the 2000 hit movie *Traffic*), are now gone. Cooperation with Colombia is increasing too. What's this going to do to the drug-trafficking industry? Being a big drug trafficker is not as beneficial as it once was. There may be **economies of scale** in transporting the drugs, but the **diseconomies of scale** have become more important because the big "firms" are visible to the more vigilant antidrug enforcers. Increased enforcement gives a relative advantage to smaller drug runners. This means that instead of a few big cartels, we will see smaller "firms." Since the smaller traffickers are less efficient, this will raise prices. That should reduce the amount of drugs demanded. But since the market demand for drugs is not infinitely elastic, killing off the big traffickers will not kill off the industry; it will just make it somewhat smaller, with smaller traffickers.

> *Q: Draw the **long-run average cost** curve before and after the increased government antidrug efforts. Show what happens to the equilibrium of supply and demand in this market as a result of the extra enforcement.*

11.15

Prostitution is illegal in Nevada, but a private "dance" in a conventioneer's hotel room is not. For the person who organizes groups of "dancers" in Las Vegas this is a good business; one fellow reports profits of $20,000 a month as his share of the take. That's a very good rate of pay for a job that requires few skills. Not surprisingly, the profits have attracted competitors who are now using modern means to break into the market: They're hacking into the local phone system to divert customers' calls from his dancers' phone numbers to their own. Hiring a competent hacker is expensive, but with the lure of large profits in a business with no obvious barriers to entry, trying to eat away some of these **economic profits** is a sensible business move.

> *Q: What would happen to the number of firms if the state of Nevada were to outlaw dancing in hotel rooms? What would happen to the profits of surviving firms?*

11.16

March 31, 2002—The Enron bankruptcy did not mark the end of the energy-trading industry. The product still exists: Enron helped create a market for complex financial products that involve futures prices of various energy commodities. Indeed, with Enron's demise the survivors in the industry have benefited. My cousin, who runs a small energy-trading business, reports that his company has been doing better than ever since the Enron bankruptcy. This is not surprising: If a competitor disappears from a market and there's no fundamental change in demand in the industry, the surviving firms will profit. The dynamics of competitive industries mean that some firms die while others flourish. The only difficulty for my cousin will come if his profits and those of other survivors attract new competitors. His current success may regrettably only be temporary.

> *Q:* *What would happen to output and price in the short run, and in the long run, if investors, totally disgusted by the Enron debacle, reduced their willingness to buy the kinds of financial derivatives in which Enron, and my cousin, have specialized?*

11.17

The first commercial egg bank—which will store unfertilized human ova—will open. Why didn't this industry exist before? Demand and costs. Demand has increased. The story talks about the growing number of women in their mid-thirties who are purposely childless but may want to have a child later on. The technology for operating the bank has been available for a while, but **long-run average cost** has been declining. The conjunction of these two events has given rise to this new industry. Shocks to demand or cost change the equilibrium price, quantity, and number and size of firms in an existing industry, but they also can call into being a new industry—or they can kill off an existing industry (for example, the buggy-whip industry).

> *Q:* *List two other completely new industries that have come into existence during your lifetime. List two others that have disappeared during your lifetime.*

11.18

April 17, 2002—Since the wave of suicide bombings in Israel began there has been a huge decline in the number of restaurant and coffeehouse customers. The owners of a coffeehouse report that they have added security guards and are including a surcharge for security on each customer's bill to cover the $3,000 in monthly security costs. Workers don't want to risk their lives as waitpersons in these places, and that has driven up labor costs and thus average cost. The owners claim they will not close, will not let the terrorists force them out of business. Perhaps not. But with demand down and costs up in what has to be a competitive industry (there are lots of restaurants and coffeehouses in each town), some are going to close. For the survivors prices will rise to cover the higher operating costs. An additional cost of the bombings to Israeli society will be higher prices for restaurant meals.

Q: Discuss which restaurants and coffeehouses will be the ones that survive this change in the equilibrium.

CHAPTER 12

Social Optima

12.1

At lunch a high-paid colleague stood up and said he was going to buy an ice cream. I asked him if he would buy a chocolate-chip cookie for me. He did, and I offered him the dollar it cost when he returned with it. He refused to take my dollar, and I felt very guilty about this. A young colleague, not so well paid, said he would be happy to take my dollar, so I gave it to him. This was clearly **Pareto-improving**: I assuaged my guilt, the young colleague now had a dollar that he did not previously have, and the high-paid colleague must have been at least as well off, or he wouldn't have refused to take my dollar.

> *Q: Is an action Pareto-improving independent of past behavior? If I had known from his past behavior that the high-paid colleague would refuse my dollar, do you think that would I have let him buy me the cookie?*

12.2

This morning there were even more deer than usual grazing on people's lawns and shrubs. (Last Saturday I saw a ten-point buck in our heavily urbanized area.) Why not allow people to shoot them, thereby increasing the food supply, decreasing the costs of maintaining shrubs and lawns, and providing sport for the residents? The city could even sell hunting licenses and be able to reduce taxes while still balancing its budget. Wouldn't this represent a gain in **efficiency**—cheap venison, too, in the middle of Austin, a city of 750,000 people?

*Q: Give some reasons why the city might not want to increase economic efficiency in this way, why allowing hunting of urban deer might not be **Pareto-improving.***

12.3

There's a new device selling for $49.99 that allows you to "clean up" the PG-13 or R-rated movies that you rent so that you or your kids won't be offended by the language, violence, and nudity. Although the device might seem like a way of imposing censorship, it should allow an improvement in well-being for everyone and thus be **Pareto-improving.** Those who want to censor movies will be happier and will be able to rent things they otherwise wouldn't. More important, directors and producers should have more freedom to make movies the way they want, since there should be less pressure on them from professional censors.

Q: Televisions are now sold with a "V chip" that allows parents to censor shows so that their children cannot view objectionable material. Does the V chip create the same potential Pareto improvements as this new invention? Why or why not?

12.4

Driving by a high school, I noticed that the only commercial establishment near it, in what is otherwise a residential area, was an office of orthodontists. The same thing was true near the middle school my sons attended. This is a very neat example of choice of location: The orthodontists locate near the clients. This minimizes costs to the clients (and to society), and the use of the land for this purpose represents a socially efficient allocation.

Q: List other examples in which professionals in one occupation congregate together in a particular location because of proximity to the client base.

12.5

We were proud sponsors of a concert. When the concert was advertised, we bought two good tickets for it, only to be told that because we had paid to sponsor it, we got two equally good "free tickets." What to do with the extra pair of tickets? We offered the free tickets to various friends, two of whom finally accepted. One friend thanked me profusely. I wanted to tell her that this was a **Pareto-improving** exchange. We get no satisfaction from the extra tickets and are thus no worse off if she takes the tickets, but she is better off going to the concert. (She must be; she chose to take the tickets from us.) Indeed, if we feel **altruistic,** we too are better off.

> *Q: If the friend knows that I get pleasure from making her better off, why doesn't she insist that I should also pay her a few dollars? If she did this, compared to the situation when I didn't give her the ticket, would the exchange still represent a Pareto improvement?*

12.6

Before class a student asked, "Can you pass out the problem set assignments far ahead of time? I like to have them before I begin to read the chapters." I asked other students if they wanted them early, and no one said yes. I then asked the other students if they would object to having them way ahead of time. No one objected. Therefore, the only person left in "society" who might be affected by this change is me, the instructor. Since I have the assignments ready two weeks before they are due, it doesn't hurt me to give them out early. The young woman who asked for the problem sets will be helped, and nobody will be hurt if I hand them out early. This is clearly a **Pareto improvement,** so I will start doing it.

> *Q: Suppose I took a vote and a majority, but not all of the students, voted in favor of handing out the problem sets early, but some voted no. Would it represent a Pareto improvement if I went ahead and handed them out?*

12.7

Vignette 5.15 describes the benefits of switching from a system in which each faculty member in a department took as many professional trips as he or she could get the department chair to pay for to a system costing the same in total but with each person limited to a fixed budget of $750. Overall this made the department chair's life easier, and it also raised the well-being of the average faculty members, since they were now free to spend the money on any kind of professional travel that they felt was valuable. But was this change a **Pareto improvement?** No. Before this change a few faculty members were taking many trips costing far more in total than $750 per year. Under the new system those faculty members were restricted to fewer trips than before. They did now have freedom of choice about their travels, but that freedom gave them an outcome that was inferior to what they had before. While society (the department as a whole) was better off, their being worse off ensured that this was not a Pareto improvement.

> *Q: If each faculty member gets $750 per year for travel, can the chair make a Pareto improvement and still cut the total budget for travel?*

12.8

March 10, 2002—The long lines at airport security are prompting the airlines and some federal agencies to propose issuing some frequent travelers "trusted traveler" cards that would speed them through security checks. Assume that these cards could not be stolen or forged (maybe they would have a thumbprint or even a retina print). Resources would not be wasted screening people who are certain not to be terrorists; those people's time would be saved, and with them whisked through security, other people would get through faster too. This would seem to be a **Pareto improvement:** So long as each inspection of other travelers (the nontrusted travelers?) doesn't take any longer than before, nobody seems to be made worse off. As often happens, though, an increase in **efficiency** might come at the cost of a reduction in **equity.** With these cards the federal government is creating a privileged class of travelers. In a world with no envy the other travelers (the nontrusted travelers) wouldn't mind this; remember, they would save time. But envy is a basic human emotion, and the federal government does not want to generate envy by creating a class of privileged travelers. It's one thing for the airlines to do this (with special check-in lines for frequent flyers) but quite another for a democratic government to do it.

> *Q: Some universities create honors sections of introductory eco-*
> *nomics, with the top professors teaching those sections and the*
> *lesser professors or teaching assistants handling the standard sec-*
> *tions. Does the existence of this two-tiered system create the same*
> *issues as in this vignette, or are the issues different?*

12.9

After using the same textbook for many years, I decided to adopt a different one for next fall's 500-student class. The bookseller was in my office, and she and her boss said I had "made their week." They were really happy about this, since their pay depends in part on what they sell. I was happy too, as I like the new book and will get pleasure from trying something new. I think my students will be better off too. This would seem like a **Pareto improvement** because everyone's better off. It isn't: The young woman who sells the book I had been using is worse off for sure. With fewer of her books sold, her bonus next year will be smaller. Pareto improvements are relatively uncommon.

> *Q: So one person is worse off, but think how many are better off.*
> *Isn't that a Pareto improvement? Why or why not?*

12.10

The student newspaper has a story about professor–student sexual relationships. As a free-market economist, I ask: Aren't these relationships **Pareto-improving**? After all, if they are consensual, both parties must be better off. This glib answer is wrong for two reasons. Even if the parties had equal power, there are third parties involved: Other students feel slighted when the professor's preferred student is treated differently from them. It's not just envy; it's the possibility that if there is a grading curve or if class time is offered (for example, to present a term paper), the other students suffer. The power is not, however, equal: The student's success in class, in the major, or in a career is controlled or at least influenced by the professor. The power relationship is inherently unequal, so the exchange is inherently not free.

> *Q: How about relationships between professors and former students who are still enrolled? Would they be Pareto-improving? How about relationships between professors and former students who have left the university?*

CHAPTER 13

Monopoly and Monopolistic Competition

13.1

While sitting on a plane today I started talking with a guy who is a pilot for a company that offers "fractional ownership" of small jets. This industry, which got started in the early 1990s, consists of a few companies that own fleets of these planes and sell shares to businesses and individuals. A one-sixteenth share, typically the smallest possible, guarantees the purchaser the rights to a certain number of hours of airplane time per year. All expenses, including pilots and maintenance, are typically covered. This allows customers to avoid the problems of safety inspections, arranging for pilots, training, and much else. Why didn't this business spring into being before the 1990s? The answer lies in the need for a large market to make it profitable. Without a large enough fleet and customer base, offering a guarantee of airplane time on demand would require charging a huge price per hour, since much of the fleet would remain idle lots of the time. Clearly too, this is not an industry that will be characterized by perfect competition. Entry barriers are likely to be quite high, so only a **monopolist** will be able to survive.

> *Q: What are the **fixed costs** in an industry like this? What are the **variable costs**? Which are likely to be higher?*

13.2

October 8, 2001—I flew home from the Dallas–Fort Worth airport last night. Having gotten to DFW two hours ahead of schedule, I hoped to get the American Airlines 6:45 PM flight instead of the 9 PM flight that I was on. However, since September 11 the 6:45 flight doesn't exist anymore.   On the other hand, it looks like American canceled very few flights from Dallas to Chicago, Seattle, and a number of other cities. (Of course too, the flight at 9 PM to Austin was overbooked.) Why the difference? Might it be that American has essentially a **monopoly** on the DFW–Austin route, while it is one of several competitors on the other routes? The company is restricting supply in a market where it is a **monopolist**.

> *Q: List some other ways in which the airline's practice might differ on its monopolized routes compared to those where it faces substantial competition?*

13.3

October 23, 2001—Another thought on the Cipro issue. On this evening's news Bayer (the drug's manufacturer) made it clear that it would be happier to sell the drug at a much lower price than it now sells it instead of giving up, even temporarily, its patent rights. Why? The **marginal cost** of producing Cipro is tiny; the **variable cost** of producing a drug is small compared to the **fixed cost** that goes into bringing it to market. If Bayer gives up its patent rights, it risks losing all of its future profits. A low current price is still above the **average variable cost** of the drug. This is a smart move for Bayer.

> *Q: Assume that the companies could not patent drugs but that the cost structure (high fixed cost, low variable cost) was the same as it is now. What would the drug market look like (quantity, quality, and price)?*

13.4

Your main text is one of around thirty economics principles books. These books appear in new editions every two or three years. Why? Partly because the material becomes obsolete fairly fast. But if that were the sole cause, we wouldn't also see new editions of basic math books every few years: It's hard to believe that college math changes every three years. Frequent new editions also can't stem from the used-book market killing off sales of new copies: If that were true, the book publishers would price high enough to account for the multiple resales of each new copy. Anyway, in economics the three-year cycle started before there was much of a used-book market. The best explanation is a combination of the partial obsolescence of the material and the need for the **monopolistic competitors** to **differentiate the product** from its competitors by adding new bells and whistles in new editions. Each book tries to carve out a niche in the market in terms of difficulty of presentation and style of approach. When another book in that niche adds a new feature—online updates, interactive CD-ROMs, or whatever—its competitors must update their editions to remain viable. If there were no obsolescence of the material, new editions might not come so frequently. But the books would still be revised regularly as a competitive response to the revisions of the slightly differentiated products with which they compete.

> *Q: The decision to assign the texts is made by your professor. If students could choose the book, would they choose an old edition or a new edition? Why? Would the cycle of new editions be as rapid as it now is?*

13.5

AT&T is raising the fees charged to long-distance customers who make out-of-state phone calls. The carrier said its plunging consumer long-distance **revenues** left it with no choice but to raise customer fees earmarked for the Federal Communication Commission's universal service fund. AT&T is far from being the only long-distance carrier using land-based lines, and it also must compete with services that offer long-distance telephoning on cell phones. Despite this, it is raising the fee, implying that it believes that it won't lose much revenue from the fee increase (that it has an **inelastic demand** at the current price). Is the demand as inelastic as AT&T's behavior implies it believes it to be, or will AT&T instead find that with the higher fees it actually collects less revenue for this purpose?

> *Q: How might AT&T's best decision about raising fees vary if MCI, Sprint, and others were to go out of business?*

13.6

All the big computer manufacturers—Dell, Gateway, Compaq, Hewlett-Packard, IBM—have little "Intel Inside" logos (with their annoying five-note sound at the end) in their television advertisements. Intel subsidizes these advertisements if the companies include this logo. Other chip makers have urged **antitrust** agencies to restrict what they argue is simply a form of tied sale. **Tied sales**—a company's using its **monopoly** power in one market to enhance its position in another, competitive market—are generally illegal. Are Intel's **subsidies** a form of tying, or are they just rebates to the purchasers of chips? In both the United States and the European Union these lawsuits have gone nowhere, with the antitrust agencies eventually dropping them. This rejection seems like a good policy decision: While Intel does have a huge share of the market for chips, there is no competitive market into which it is trying to spill over its monopoly power.

> *Q: Even though Intel may not be engaging in anticompetitive behavior by tying two products, can you argue that its behavior represents an anticompetitive practice in the chip market itself— an attempt to crowd out AMD, Cyrix, and the other small processor manufacturers? Or is it just a way of offering a volume discount to purchasers of the chips?*

13.7

Currently in the United States if you switch cell phone carriers, your old telephone number dies and you must get a new one. It would be a tremendous hassle to have to tell all your potential callers that your number has changed, so this requirement creates a "lock-in effect": It ties users to the cell phone company they signed up with. It gives your existing cell phone carrier short-term **monopoly** power over you. Under the Telecommunications Act of 1996 cellular phone carriers are not supposed to do this, but they have repeatedly and successfully lobbied the Federal Communications Commission to postpone enforcing that provision of the act. The losers are the consumers—unless they were so smart that they always chose the best firm when they obtained their phones. The winners are the companies that got into the cell phone business early and locked in customers. Even these quasi-monopolists, however, face limits: If they raise price too far above cost, new entrants can attract business by lowering their prices enough to attract customers willing to endure the hassle of getting a new cell phone number.

> *Q: Try estimating the cost—the hassle—to you of switching the number of your cell phone. Then ask yourself how good a deal a competing company would have to give you on your monthly rate before you would be willing to incur this cost. What are the characteristics of people who are more likely, and less likely, to switch?*

13.8

In the last few years U.S. television shows have been swamped with ads for prescription drugs. Since consumers cannot buy these drugs directly, the ads are intended to induce you to pester your physician to prescribe the drug for you—for things such as anxiety, depression, impotence, and heartburn. One company recently advertised that its new drug is better than the one it has been advertising for many years. Why suddenly campaign against its own drug, and why try to get consumers to ask their doctors to switch? The reason is simple: The patent on the old drug runs out this year, and its price will plummet as other companies are allowed to produce and sell the drug in what will become a highly competitive market. The new ads are a way of building loyalty to a new, monopolized brand at a time when the old **monopoly** will disappear.

> *Q: Microsoft introduces new operating systems for personal computers every three or four years. How is that behavior similar to or different from the introduction of the new drug described here?*

13.9

A recent television ad for Depends, the protective underwear for senior citizens, asked, "How to improve the protection of Depends? Lower the price!" Presumably the ad means that people can now buy more of the product and thus get more protection. This is true as long as Depends does not have a completely **inelastic demand.** But even if the demand were somewhat inelastic, the company would not lower its price, as **revenue** would drop while the **total cost** of production would rise. It must be the case that the manufacturer believes that it has a highly **elastic demand** (appropriately enough for underwear). Its managers must think that the price cut will generate such a large increase in quantity sold that revenue will rise more than enough to offset the increase in total cost. A more accurate ad thus would ask, "How to improve the protection of Depends *a lot*? Lower the price!"

> *Q: Even before any extra Depends are sold the new advertising campaign costs the company money. How does this cost affect the **price elasticity of demand** that is required before it will pay the company to lower the price?*

13.10

A local grocery store has a truly immense array of famous brands of beer from all over the world, with lots of examples of microbrews from all regions of the United States. How can a small brand stand out from the shelves against all this competition? In other words, how can the manufacturer practice **product differentiation** and get the customer's attention? These companies have no national advertising budgets; they are not sponsoring the Super Bowl. The trick appears to be some clever eye-catching name. Years ago we saw "Black Dog" and "Pete's Wicked Ale." Today we have "Arrogant Bastard Ale," a fairly heavy brew whose label tells the customer that he or she probably isn't tough enough to drink this bottle and should instead buy one of the wimpy standard brands with a multimillion-dollar advertising budget. That is a clever name and a clever challenge. While I didn't buy a bottle, it has stuck in my mind and probably will win me over the next time I shop.

> *Q: Think up a name for a brand of beer that you will create. The only requirements are that your brand name cannot be unprintable in a family newspaper (not a very stringent standard today) and must be the best possible name to sell more of the beer.*

13.11

A colleague commented on Vignette 10.10 about Viagra, remarking that drugstores sell a product called Niag*a*ra that claims to have similar effects. The product's name has now been changed to Nexcite. There are a number of reasons for the name change, but the main reason probably is that Niagara was sued or threatened with suit for trademark infringement by the manufacturers of the **monopolized** product Viagra. This is a pretty clear-cut case: The products are supposed to do the same thing, and a well-known trademark name is being appropriated to compete against its owner. But what if a new company in a totally different product market uses or refers to a trademark, in no way trying to compete in a legally monopolized market? One might argue that there's no problem, since there is no loss of sales by the company owning the trademark. The new company, though, is trying to make profits by using the older company's investment in its brand name. The owner doesn't lose anything in its original market, but the action is tantamount to stealing the fruits of someone else's investment.

> *Q: Johnny Carson, a popular television host in the 1970s and 1980s, was introduced every night by his sidekick yelling, "Here's Johnny!" During the 1980s a portable toilet company used the phrase as the name for its product. Carson sued and succeeded in stopping the company from using this name. How is the Carson case different from the Niagara case? How is it the same?*

13.12

It's tough to be a **monopolist.** Witness the continuing efforts of the diamond **monopoly**—De Beers Consolidated and its Central Selling Organization—to make sure that people continue buying diamond jewelry and do not sell the diamond jewelry they already own. De Beers has a new TV ad for a "three-diamond" ring and even has a new piece of music to replace the pseudo-baroque theme it has been using for at least ten years. These endeavors follow its efforts to lure more established families into buying a second diamond (a twenty-fifth wedding anniversary token of love) and its successful expansion of the diamond ring as a wedding token to newly affluent Asian countries. De Beers's main problem is not so much its potential competitors, although new diamond discoveries outside its control do pose continual concerns. Instead, it is the need, faced by every monopolist, to make sure that the **demand curve** is pushed out as far as it can be.

> *Q: Would you buy your fiancée (or let your fiancé buy you) a turquoise engagement ring? What would happen to De Beers, which would remain the diamond monopolist, if people began accepting turquoise as a substitute for diamonds?*

13.13

If I use my computer (running Microsoft Windows 2000) for more than a week without rebooting, my version of Netscape begins to give me difficulties. First it operates very slowly, and then it stops responding. I've tried using Explorer, also a Microsoft product, and have had no such problems. I'm sure the folks at Microsoft would love me to switch away from Netscape. Even if they don't formally **tie** together their Web browser to the Windows operating system, which they monopolize, they can structure the codes to make the operating system more compatible with Explorer than with the competing Netscape without violating any judgments or settlements of the long-running **antitrust** suit brought against them. I'm not ready to switch to Explorer, but if Microsoft succeeds in making its next-generation operating system even less compatible with Netscape, I'll probably, and sadly, have to switch.

> *Q: Is the consumer worse off if Microsoft ties its operating system to its Web browser? What loss, if any, is inflicted on the consumer by this practice?*

13.14

The old James Bond movie *Live and Let Die* begins with a funeral procession in New Orleans. In the movie Mr. Big, the chief villain, hatches a scheme to give heroin away—free—in the United States. The purpose of this plan is to drive out his competitors. Once he has succeeded in monopolizing the market, he plans to raise prices to their **monopoly** level. He implicitly believes that the short-run losses he incurs by giving the drug away will be more than made up for by the monopoly profits he will make once his competitors have been driven out of the market. His predatory pricing—selling below **average variable cost**—makes sense only if he can survive those losses better than his competitors can, and if he believes it will be difficult for new competitors to come into the market. If he's correct, he will reap monopoly profits for a long time.

> *Q: Will Mr. Big's plan work better if the demand for heroin is inelastic or if it's elastic?*

13.15

April 2, 2002—This summer the cost of a first-class stamp is being raised from thirty-four to thirty-seven cents. To maintain demand the U.S. Postal Service (USPS) has undertaken a new advertising campaign. I doubt that advertising will help much, at least not in the part of its business involving letters and bills. The problem is that the long-run cost of transmitting paper documents is rising, while the long-run cost of transmitting electrons (fax, e-mails, electronic funds transfers) is falling. The cost of a one-minute fax has fallen below ten cents at the same time that stamp prices have risen. Until the 1980s we mailed checks every month for the phone, electricity, gas, and mortgage. We now have these all directly debited; it's easier, and the companies save money this way too. The only hope for the USPS in the long run is in its lines of business where goods must be sent: parcels and express mail. Whether it is efficient enough to compete in these areas with FedEx, UPS, Airborne, and others is another question.

> *Q: The USPS has a **monopoly** on sending letters. Why doesn't that monopoly guarantee it **economic profits** forever?*

13.16

The Wall Street Journal has a story about the expansion of the Ritz-Carlton luxury hotel chain. The company has a **monopoly** on its prestigious name; indeed, the word *ritzy* has become an adjective denoting "snobbish" or "fancy." The problem is that the company has trouble maintaining the quality of the services offered in all the hotels that it has decided to create worldwide. This is a common problem for businesses and organizations: There is a **trade-off** between maximizing profits by exploiting a prestige name and letting the expansion diminish the prestige for all of a business's units. As the firm moves down its quantity **demand curve,** it becomes increasingly difficult to maintain the quality of each unit. Its demand curve shifts leftward, reducing its **revenue** at each quantity. Ritz-Carlton should expand until the reduction in profits resulting from lower quality and loss of reputation exceeds the gain in profits from opening another hotel that exploits the company's reputation.

> *Q: Is this problem specific to Ritz-Carlton? Might a company like McDonald's have similar problems? What can Ritz-Carlton or McDonald's do to reduce these difficulties?*

13.17

Two of my economics major students were commenting on how good the food is at the privately run food stand on campus and how they hoped that the young immigrant who runs it makes lots of money. I hope not, and I bet not. The university leases the rights to set up a stand in that location. The university has a **monopoly** on the space on campus, while the number of potential bidders to operate food stands is large. If the officials who determine which stands can be operated are clever, they should extract from the winning bidder all profits above what he or she would earn in a competitive market. The winner would make just enough to cover capital costs and the **opportunity cost** of labor time. If the university does not receive this much from the lease it writes, then it will be sharing its monopoly profits with the operator of the food stand. It will be reducing the university's **revenue** and hurting the citizens, who pay taxes to the state that supports the university, and the students who pay tuition.

> *Q: Are there any reasons why the university might not want to push the winning bidder down to zero **economic profits**?*

13.18

Governments create some **monopolies.** One of the most widespread monopolies is religion. Many countries, including Great Britain, have established religions that receive government aid and are favored in other ways. Economic thinking suggests that in a market where there is a monopoly—where there is only one kind of product—the total amount consumed will be smaller than otherwise. This seems to be the case for religion too. A recent study that used data for fifty-nine countries in 1997 finds that among countries that are otherwise identical in terms of level of economic development, weekly church attendance is 17 percentage points lower in countries where the government fosters a particular religion. It's not that the government-sponsored religion charges too high a price; instead, it often doesn't exhibit the innovations and product diversity that consumers of religion desire.

> *Q: Given this discussion, what would you think of a proposal to amend the U.S. Constitution to make Christianity the national religion, able to receive government aid not available to other religions?*

13.19

The Wall Street Journal reports on a "problem" facing a number of famous northeastern prep schools. Less wealthy schools that play in the same basketball league have been recruiting potential basketball stars and destroying teams from Exeter, Phillips, Choate, and their peers. The administrators at these schools don't like the embarrassment of fifty-point losses and have proposed the creation of a new league that would exclude the upstarts. In essence, they wish to banish competition by offering a differentiated product—a well-financed education with implicit limits on basketball prowess—from what the less famous schools offer. This is standard economic behavior: If you are losing out in a market, use **product differentiation** and try to exclude the "firms" that previously had a competitive advantage.

> *Q: Suppose you were the athletic director at one of these elite schools. Provide arguments in favor of banning the upstarts from your league that might appear less narrow-minded.*

13.20

Between 2000 and 2001 the average price of a ticket to a rock concert rose much more rapidly than did the rate of inflation. At the same time, total rock ticket **revenue** fell. It's possible that the **monopoly** promoters of rock concerts raised prices to the point where they had an **elastic demand,** so they lost more revenue from audience members who stayed away from concerts than they gained from the higher prices paid by audiences that continued attending. Alternatively, perhaps the mild economic recession of 2001 reduced the demand for rock concerts generally. With just this information it's hard to tell whether the monopoly promoters followed the correct pricing strategy.

*Q: If you were a monopoly seller of rock concert tickets and believed that the decline in revenue had occurred because you had moved onto the elastic part of your **demand curve**, what would you do with the ticket price? If you believed it was caused by the recession, what would you do with the ticket price?*

CHAPTER 14

Price Discrimination

14.1

The local video store charges the same rental price for a DVD as it does for a videocassette. The **marginal cost** of producing another copy of a movie on DVD is no greater than the marginal cost of producing another videocassette copy. Unlike the video, the DVD should last forever, and so the store should be able to rent it out many more times than it can rent out the video. DVDs can be stored in less shelf space than videos. The **average total cost** to the video store per rental is thus lower on DVDs, so why don't rental prices reflect this cost difference? Eventually they will be cheaper; since the rental market is competitive, DVD rental prices will someday reflect the lower **long-run average cost.** Right now—in the short run—the people who have DVD players are generally wealthier customers who have an **inelastic demand** for rentals. This gives the video stores, and the producers who sell the new videos and DVDs to the stores, the temporary ability to **price discriminate;** they have a short-run **monopoly.** They can charge a higher markup to DVD users, at least until DVDs become more widely owned.

> *Q: If you are operating a store, are looking for profitable new lines of business, and know that the video stores discriminate against owners of DVD players, what can you do to take advantage of the situation described here?*

14.2

While visiting a Dutch university a few years ago I wanted to buy a cup of coffee. The choice was the cafeteria or a vending machine in the same building. The cafeteria was open, so I bought my cup there. At 7 PM I went back to buy another cup. The cafeteria was closed, so I went to the vending machine. The price for a cup of coffee was higher than it had been during the day; the vending machine was programmed to require a higher price at times when there was no competition from the cafeteria. The cost of restocking and servicing the coffee machine doesn't depend on when the vending machine coffee was consumed. The vending machine company price discriminates by charging a lot when the substitute—the cafeteria—isn't available, when there is an **inelastic demand** for the vending machine's coffee. It prices lower when the cafeteria is open—when demand is more **elastic**.

> *Q:*   *How would you behave if your dormitory installed variable-price vending machines near the cafeteria and charged higher prices on food when the cafeteria is closed?*

14.3

A student mentioned the small seasonal business he runs. He picks up your used Christmas tree, throws it into his pickup truck, and disposes of it for you. The Christmas trees differ little in size, but he charges a higher price if the distance from the house to the street is longer so that he has to work harder. This is surely cost-based **price discrimination.** He also mentioned, though, that he once charged a higher price to a woman in curlers and slippers. He figured that she was much less willing to drag the tree by herself than were most of his customers. Believing she had an **inelastic demand,** he quoted her a higher price than usual. This probably would be illegal or at least severely frowned upon for a larger business, but it is a good example of demand-based price discrimination.

> *Q:*   *If he believed she had an inelastic demand, why didn't he charge her $500 for the service? What does your answer say about how the **price elasticity of demand** changes as the price of the service changes?*

14.4

A recent economic study compared prices of the same sets of goods, some purchased in stores and others purchased over the

Web. On the goods that were purchased in stores, women and minorities paid about 1 to 2 percent more than white males did. There were no differences in the prices paid by women and minorities compared to white men on goods that were purchased over the Web. Does the anonymity of Web purchases prevent sellers from separating markets and **price discriminating,** as the authors claimed? Or are the women and minorities who shop over the Web more clever consumers relative to white males than are those who shop in stores?

> *Q:* *If this is discrimination, is it discrimination based on differences in costs of production or discrimination based on differences in the* ***price elasticity of demand****?*

14.5

The second telephone line that we recently got rid of cost, as I remember, more than did a single line. Why should that be? Surely the phone company can install and service the second line at lower **average total cost** than it can service just one line. It might be due to regulatory restrictions, but it could also be that it is pure demand-based **price discrimination:** Those customers who want a second line have a more **inelastic demand** for it (perhaps partly because they have higher incomes) than do those who want just one line.

> *Q:* *Think about your parents' house. If they have two phone lines, why? How has their interest in having a second phone line been affected by the advent of cable modems?*

14.6

The Office Depot catalog has an advertisement for two sizes of fax paper, each the same width but one forty-nine feet long for $12.99 for two rolls and the other ninety-eight feet long for $11.99 a roll. Assuming this is not a typographical error, how could this be? It might be cost-based **price discrimination:** It could be that while the **marginal cost** of the smaller roll is lower, there are **fixed costs** of making and inventorying what might be an unusual product. I doubt that the higher price of the smaller rolls is due to demand-based price discrimination. It might be true that people who can use only the smaller roll have a less **elastic demand** for fax paper, but the product is sold in a highly competitive market, thus destroying an essential precondition for the existence of demand-based price discrimination, namely, that the seller **monopolize** the product.

> *Q: If the difference in the prices of the two products is cost-based, what will happen to the difference if consumers respond to advertisements like this by buying one ninety-eight-foot roll instead of two forty-nine-foot rolls?*

14.7

The Wall Street Journal has a story about guys buying panty hose—men who want warmth and/or support for their leg muscles. Currently the price of men's panty hose (made with flies in front) exceeds that of women's panty hose. Does this reflect discrimination against men, the reverse of the discrimination often claimed by women in such markets as dry cleaning and clothing? Possibly. It may be that men's demand (to the extent that there is any) is less elastic than that of women. It is more likely, though, that the discrimination is cost-based: Men's panty hose require more material, and because demand is relatively small, manufacturers may be unable to take advantage of **economies of scale** in production, distribution, and inventorying.

> *Q: What does this suggest will happen to the price of men's panty hose compared to women's as more men start wearing panty hose?*

14.8

There are many cases where new customers get a better deal than old customers do. This is true for sales from the Victoria's Secret catalog: The company's computerized records tell it when you last bought. The catalog offers lower prices if your last purchase was a long time ago. Similarly, this week Roadrunner cable modems are offering a $19.95 monthly price for three months (instead of the usual $44.95) if you sign on now. Both represent good examples of pure demand-based **price discrimination:** The good or service offered is identical, and the only difference between customers is how wedded to the good or service they appear to be. The companies assume that frequent buyers or long-term users will buy anyway and thus they have an **inelastic demand.** Another precondition for price discrimination is met too: The companies are sure beforehand that the low-priced good or service—the lingerie or the high-speed Internet connection—will not be resold.

Q: We don't see this kind of pricing behavior by auto retailers. Why not?

14.9

Maybe it makes sense to look into buying higher-octane gas instead of regular 87-octane gas. The prices of 89-octane and 93-octane gas are fourteen cents and twenty cents above that of the 87-octane gas at my local station, differences that seem typical of those around town. Does this difference reflect cost-based **price discrimination?** Or is it demand-based price discrimination? Experts on the industry tell me that the difference in the **marginal cost** of production between 87- and 93-octane gas is about five cents. Most of the price difference is due to demand-based price discrimination. My car takes any kind of gasoline, so I can choose which type to buy. But some car owners are locked into the higher-octane gasoline: Their demand is necessarily less elastic, as they do not have a choice about whether to buy low-octane gas. Still other drivers mistakenly think that their autos, which will run perfectly well on low-octane gas, will run better with higher-octane gasoline. They have an **inelastic demand** because of their incorrect beliefs.

Q: What would be the effect on the price differences for the different octane gasolines if a consumer group launched a publicity campaign demonstrating that most cars run just as well on lower-octane gas?

14.10

People wanted the state of Florida to investigate why a five-pound package of matzo (unleavened Passover bread) that sold for $4.98 in Brooklyn, New York, sold for $11.99 in Boca Raton, Florida. Does this price difference reflect differences in underlying costs, or might it be demand-based **price discrimination?** Most of the matzo is made in the New York area or is imported from Israel, but it's hard to believe that transportation costs are high enough to account for the difference in prices. A better explanation is the nature of the clientele: In a Florida market consisting of many older people there may be less shopping around and less information about prices than in New York. Also, in the more densely populated New York market it is easier to search for better deals. Both of these facts mean that there is a more **elastic demand** for matzo in New York than in Florida. Firms in Florida can take advantage of the relatively **inelastic demand** by charging higher prices than their New York counterparts charge.

> *Q: Let's say you run a bakery and notice this huge difference in prices. Wouldn't competition lead you to enter the matzo market to get some of these excess profits during the eight-day Passover period?*

14.11

Resident undergrads at the University of Texas at Austin pay $84 per credit hour; nonresidents pay $295, roughly three and a half times as much. Why does the university **price discriminate,** since the **marginal cost** of educating in-state and out-of-state students is about the same? One rationale is **equity:** Parents of in-state students pay the taxes that cover about 20 percent of the university's costs. But out-of-state tuition seems too high to be justified on this basis alone. Instead, it's a way that the state raises **revenue**—it represents demand-based price discrimination. The university is not a **monopoly,** but it does have some monopoly power. Out-of-state students who are especially interested in the fun of being in Austin, Texas, or who want a particular major that the university is very good in (petroleum engineering, for example) are willing to pay the high tuition. A very large fraction of out-of-state students say that there is something very special about the university that attracted them (and that made them willing to pay this high tuition).

> *Q: What does this discussion suggest will be true about the mix of in-state and out-of-state hotel majors at Michigan State University, one of the few institutions to offer a hotel management major?*

14.12

Verdi's opera *Rigoletto* includes a character who is a professional assassin. He tells the court jester Rigoletto, who would like to have the Duke, his employer, assassinated, "[I'm] an expert swordsman . . . a man who'll rid you of a rival for a pittance." Rigoletto asks, "For a nobleman, how much would you require?" The assassin answers, "That would be somewhat higher." Why does the assassin charge more for killing a nobleman? Is it cost-based **price discrimination?** Is killing a nobleman riskier in the sense that the likelihood of being killed or caught is greater? Or is it pure price discrimination because a client who wants to have a nobleman killed has a lower **price elasticity of demand** and is thus willing to pay more than a client who wants a commoner assassinated? Both possibilities are consistent with behavior in the opera.

> *Q:* *How would you answer this question if you knew for sure that the assassin would be leaving town immediately after the deed and would never be caught?*

CHAPTER 15

Oligopoly (Including Game Theory)

15.1

One of the well-known game-theory examples is called the Battle of the Sexes game. This came to life for me one spring weekend in 1994. The movie *Little Women* had opened, and my wife desperately wanted to see it. The thought turned my stomach, especially because another, locally made movie about young women, *Teenage Catgirls in Heat,* was playing in town. My wife had no interest in seeing that. The alternative to going out was staying home and watching a *Star Trek* rerun. We would have been together watching the rerun, which was better than being separated and watching separate movies, but we wouldn't have been very happy. There is no single solution to this game, so I proposed that we alternate by seeing *Little Women* that weekend and *Catgirls* the next. This "mixed-strategy" idea is an equilibrium solution for this game. We saw *Little Women,* and my wife was happy. Regrettably, *Catgirls* never showed after that weekend and I never got to see it.

> *Q: What would the outcome have been if either my wife or I would have preferred to see the other person's movie than watch the* Star Trek *rerun?*

15.2

November 4, 2001—Since November 1, 2001, American Airlines is no longer serving meals, or even snacks, on most of its domestic flights. This change lowers its costs (and makes the refreshment service like that of Southwest Airlines, which proudly states that it gives passengers peanuts). What does the change imply about American's competitive stance vis-à-vis United, Northwest, and Delta? Will people prefer those other airlines (reducing American's **revenue**), or will those airlines also cut back on meal service?

> *Q: Getting rid of meals is clearly a competitive move. So why doesn't American Airlines also get rid of reserved seats and offer first-come, first-served seating like Southwest, which also represents a cost saving?*

15.3

Strategic Behavior on an Airplane (best understood if you draw the seat configuration of the airplane). I was sitting on an airplane going from Frankfurt, Germany, to Dallas. In the three-seat row in front of me the middle seat was empty. In the three-seat row in front of that both the middle and right-hand seats were empty. The guy in the left seat one row ahead of me moved to the center seat. The man in the right seat of that row was thus crowded, got annoyed, and moved one row forward. The piggish man then lay down and stretched out, as he now had the whole row to himself. His strategy could have failed—he might have had to spend some time in the center seat next to the other guy if the other fellow hadn't moved. But the other fellow did move, so his strategy was successful.

> *Q: Say you were the man in the right seat of the row ahead of me and you were unwilling to move and didn't like to be pushed around or liked teaching piggish people a lesson. What behavior would you have engaged in to induce the piggish man to retreat to his original seat?*

15.4

At my wife's office Christmas party they have a "Chinese gift exchange." Each person has a numbered ticket, 1 to N. Each of the N people has bought a present and wrapped it. The first person must pick one of the wrapped gifts and unwrap it. Persons 2 through N have a choice of drawing one of the wrapped gifts or taking a gift from someone who is already holding an (unwrapped) gift. The person whose gift was taken then must draw one of the wrapped gifts. This goes on until all the numbers are chosen. Player 1 then makes the final move, exchanging his or her gift for one somebody else is holding (if Player 1 wants to do this). A minor additional rule is that no gift can be grabbed more than three times. What is the optimal strategy: to draw an unopened gift or to take a gift someone else is holding? If you take a gift someone else has opened, which gift do you take? There are two unknowns: (1) the distribution of the quality of the gifts and (2) the distribution of players' tastes for the gifts. If people's tastes are all entirely different from each other, this problem is uninteresting because everybody would just as soon draw an unopened present. The same is true if all players perceive the gifts as being identical in quality.

> *Q: What would you do in this situation, draw or take someone else's gift? Why? How does you answer depend on which number you have between 1 and N?*

15.5

The local newspaper reports that the U.S. Justice Department opposes allowing American Airlines and British Airways to ally in transatlantic travel, arguing that this will give them 51 percent of market share at London's Heathrow airport. The airlines claim that the share would only be 37 percent and, more important, that the appropriate market is not just Heathrow but all European hubs. They argue that those hubs, especially Paris and Frankfurt, are controlled by other U.S–European airline alliances and that their own alliance will not give them a large share of the appropriately defined market: European hubs. This is a classic case of determining what the relevant market is in determining the potential effects of a merger.

> *Q: Give arguments to support the Justice Department's view that each local European hub constitutes a market. What evidence and data would you need to support that view?*

15.6

A Beautiful Mind, a movie starring Russell Crowe, is about John Nash, the developer of much of modern game theory. The movie has a scene that nicely illustrates the gains to cooperative strategies. Nash and four friends are in a bar, and they are eyeing the young women, one of whom is strikingly beautiful. The Nash character thinks for a minute and says to his colleagues that they should *not all* go up and ask the beautiful woman over. She will turn them down no matter what, and the other women will be offended and turn down any subsequent invitations. Instead, he proposes that they cooperate, ignore the beautiful woman, and ask the other women out. This cooperative strategy is successful— they all get dates—even though this is *not* a **Nash equilibrium.**

> *Q: Would the outcome have been the same if one of the five guys had been extremely good-looking and very personable? What might the outcome have been in that case?*

15.7

We have lots of outside speakers who visit the Economics Department and present one-and-a-half-hour seminars in which they lecture about their current research. Some seminars are expected to be excellent, while a few others are unlikely to interest more than three faculty members. To have only three faculty members show up at a seminar is an embarrassment for the department. The chair has begun to have the department's administrative assistant go around to faculty offices before the seminars he expects to be poorly attended and ask the faculty members to attend. This approach may work for a while, but once faculty members get used to it and learn to predict which seminars will generate this sort of cajoling, they will be sure to be out of their offices before the probably poorly attended seminars. The **Nash equilibrium** here is poor attendance, with most faculty members making sure to hide out to avoid the chair or his agents.

> *Q: How is this game similar to the standard **prisoners' dilemma** problem in game theory? Help the chair out by suggesting things that he can do to get the "society" (the Department of Economics) out of what appears to be a Nash equilibrium that is like a prisoners' dilemma.*

15.8

A large number of Ph.D. students who are seeking faculty jobs have their own websites. Many of the people from one particular university have posted their pictures. The first three women are extraordinarily good-looking, and the first two men are remarkably handsome. I begin to think, "In addition to producing good students this economics department also produces good-looking students." The next student, however, has no picture, and the same is true for three of the eight others. I then think that perhaps only those students who are good-looking post their pictures on the Web. But even if those without pictures were good-looking, I would infer they are ugly, since they failed to put their pictures up. If pictures are allowed and those I see are handsome or beautiful, I will always infer that those who are left out are ugly. As long as you believe that those people who don't have pictures up are on average worse-looking than you, it pays to put your own picture on your website. Once the best-looking post their pictures, it pays the next-best-looking to post his or hers, and so on. The **Nash equilibrium** of this game has everyone except the ugliest person posting his or her picture.

> *Q: Does the same behavior carry over into résumés used by college students looking for jobs when they graduate? Would you put your picture on your résumé? Why or why not? Would it be better if universities forbade students from posting pictures on their websites or résumés?*

15.9

Local television stations have been running many ads by Southwestern Bell, the regional local telephone company, for DSL lines. The reason for this deluge may be described by my household's behavior. We got rid of our second phone line, the one we had been using for a dial-up Internet connection, and had the TV cable company install a cable modem. DSL competes with cable modems, so Southwestern Bell lost business in its basic telephone line of operations when we made our decision. It also lost business in the growing market for fast Internet connections. The ads are its strategy to fight back in that market. Presumably it recognizes that the market for second telephone lines is not going to grow any more and realizes that it must expand its share of Internet connections.

> *Q: Currently cable modems are much more widespread than DSL service. That being the case, what strategies beyond advertising*

would you recommend to Southwestern Bell to expand the DSL business?

15.10

Textbook publishers employ traveling representatives who visit professors and try to get them to use their company's textbooks. In the late 1960s there were travelers from many different companies—Irwin, Addison Wesley, Scott-Foresman, Harper & Row, Houghton Mifflin, Harcourt Brace, Prentice-Hall, and many others—all competing in the economics textbook business. Today three companies account for roughly 90 percent of sales: McGrawHill/Irwin (the publisher of this book), the Pearson Group, and Thomson Learning. This is now an **oligopoly** both in terms of total market share and in terms of the companies' behavior aimed at garnering additional market share. Students complain about textbook prices, but do the prices result from large markups or from rapidly rising input costs? In any market it is impossible to determine which is happening simply by looking at rising prices; detailed cost information is required.

> *Q: Have textbook prices really increased? Two leading economics textbooks sold in 1961 for $7.50. In 2001 each sold for $115, over fifteen times as much. During the same period the Consumer Price Index, a measure of all prices facing consumers, rose by only 5.95 times (from a price of $1 to a price of $5.95). Are there reasons other than the greater oligopoly in the industry that might explain why textbook prices have risen more rapidly than inflation generally?*

15.11

Our clothes dryer died yesterday, so we went out shopping for a new one. I said we should go to Sears, but my wife thought that Sears has only its own brand (Kenmore) of appliances. I thought that that was no longer true, and I was correct: A few years ago Sears began carrying all major brands and trying to compete with the discount appliance stores. Why did they switch strategies after so many years of advertising Sears and Kenmore together? They increasingly saw their prices being undercut by discounters as customers insisted on shopping based on price instead of on brand loyalty. The only way Sears could maintain its sales against the competition was to offer a full range of choices.

> *Q: If you had a small appliance store offering exclusively May-tag appliances and saw places like Sears expanding to offer many different brands, what would you try to do to stay in business?*

15.12

I've built up a reputation for being completely, perhaps even bru-tally, honest in my recommendations for students and evalua-tions of people for jobs and promotion. Being honest in these matters is an investment in reputation: If you're honest for a while, people will believe you thereafter. The problem is that incentives may change in the final years of a career. Why main-tain a strategy of honesty when there is no future reputation to be affected? Why not be increasingly overoptimistic about students' likely future success, since by the time I'm proved wrong I won't be writing any more letters? The problem with this thinking is that the people reading the letters may be equally aware that the end is in sight for me. They will deduce my incentives to shade the letters toward excessive optimism and will pay them appro-priately little attention. Knowing that, I had better remain honest. The only way out, if I want to play this finite game, is to write glowing recommendations, make people uncertain about the end of my career, and surprise people by suddenly retiring and ceas-ing to write recommendations.

> *Q: What does this vignette tell you about which professors you should approach for recommendations for internships, jobs, and graduate school?*

15.13

The major fast-food chains seem to be unable to break the ninety-nine-cent barrier for burger prices. The standard burger price goes above $1 occasionally, and then one of the major companies begins selling "Value Meals" or the equivalent, and the others have to cut back prices to attract customers. This is classic "kinked demand curve" behavior: If you raise your price in an oligopoly and the others don't, you lose lots of sales. (If the market were competitive, you couldn't raise price at all without losing all your sales.) Both Burger King and McDonald's are not making much profit from their most famous products, the Whopper and the Big Mac. Wendy's has followed a different strategy, going for the high end by marketing quality and charging more. This strategy has paid off: Wendy's profits have grown very sharply over the last five years. Why don't McDonald's and Burger King do the same thing? Perhaps because they have marketed at the middle or lower end for so long, their advertisements for high-quality, high-end products would not be credible.

> *Q: If McDonald's advertises a new "Superburger" costing the same as Wendy's products, would you believe an advertisement trumpeting its high quality? What could McDonald's do to get you to believe the ad?*

15.14

How to Publicize This Book? The publisher will be advertising this book at conventions, in scholarly journals read by teachers of economics, and in print brochures sent to economics teachers. But I'd like to do something myself, so maybe I can send an e-mail to the people I know personally who teach introductory economics. The e-mail can't just announce the book; it also needs to provide samples of the contents as a "teaser." The problem is, What samples should I send? I face a game with the recipients, with my strategies being to send the very best vignettes or to send a random sample. Their strategies are "Believe me" and "Don't believe me." If they believe me, I might as well send and claim that I am giving a random sample, since that way they will believe they've gotten a good picture of the book. If they're not going to believe me anyway, they will assume that whatever I send overstates the quality of the book, and they will ignore it. Sending a random sample is a *dominant strategy* for me. Knowing this is true for me, the recipients of my e-mail will believe it is random too. My sending a random sample and their believing me result in a **Nash equilibrium** for this game.

> *Q: What about a third strategy for me: Pick out the most boring vignettes in the book, send them, and tell the recipients that these are the worst? Might that be a better strategy for me, or is it dominated by the random strategy proposed in this vignette?*

15.15

I'm rethinking whether I should ask for a larger advance (up-front money) from my publisher. Not that I want the money now, but as a way to get the publisher to promote the book more heavily. Vignette 9.17 makes it clear that to a competitive firm, the advance is a **fixed cost** that will not affect the publisher's subsequent advertising for the book. This publisher is hardly a competitive firm; it's an **oligopolist** in which the managers have substantial discretion. As in many firms, the internal dynamics of managerial behavior may dictate actions that are not **profit-maximizing.** One economist received immense publicity in the mid-1990s after he got a $1 million advance for his economic principles textbook. The publisher subsequently devoted tremendous resources to promoting the book, perhaps because the editors who had contracted for it had an incentive to ensure that their project generated large sales. Perhaps they even advertised so heavily that the marginal advertising dollar generated less than a dollar of extra sales. If my publisher thinks the same way—does not think marginally the way he or she should to maximize profits—a larger advance may be a good way to induce excessive advertising and generate higher sales of the book and larger royalties for me!

> *Q: If you were a stockholder in a firm that behaved in this way, how would you feel about the managers' behavior?*

15.16

The novel *Thinks . . .* by David Lodge ends with the main character, a noted adulterer, discovering that his wife is having an affair. He remarks, "It was tit for tat. She had defected knowing that he had defected." The author clearly views marriage as a repeated **prisoners' dilemma,** one in which each spouse has the strategies Cheat, Don't Cheat. He implies that the desirable equilibrium is each party choosing Don't Cheat. The hero's wife, trying to punish the hero, has chosen the strategy Cheat in the hopes of getting her husband back to the desired equilibrium. Punishment in a repeated prisoners' dilemma is a good strategy: If my rival cuts price below cost, I can do the same thing, but for a while this strategy hurts both of us. Worse still, in a marriage each party has the option of not staying around to bear the punishment: Each could file for divorce and end this most dangerous game.

> *Q: Would you be more or less careful to make sure that your spouse doesn't find out that you are cheating if divorce is a possibility?*

15.17

In Puccini's one-act opera *Gianni Schicchi*, Buoso Donati has died and left his large estate to a monastery. Before the will is read by anyone else, the relatives call in a noted mimic, Gianni Schicchi, to play Buoso on his deathbed, rewrite the will in their favor, and then convincingly die. The relatives explain to Gianni Schicchi just how severe are the penalties for tampering with a will (including having one's hand cut off). The plan is put into effect, but on the deathbed Gianni Schicchi, as Buoso Donati, rewrites the will, leaving the entire estate to the noted mimic and great artist Gianni Schicchi. The relatives can expose him, and thereby themselves too, or they can remain silent. This is a multiperiod game, and Gianni understood from the start that his best strategy is to rewrite the will to his own benefit. He knew that the relatives would refuse to expose themselves to punishment if he cheated. Gianni's behavior is **subgame perfect:** Cheating the relatives is his consistent, maximizing strategy over the entire game. The relatives did not think far enough ahead. If they had understood the incentives facing Gianni, they never would have hired him. One hopes that **oligopolists,** who play in repeated games with fellow oligopolists, are able to do better than the relatives, who failed to understand subgame perfect behavior.

> *Q: How would Gianni's behavior have differed if the laws against falsifying a will had been harsher on him than on the relatives who hired him? Would he have done the same thing, done what the relatives wanted, or found something in between to do?*

15.18

In *American Pie 2* a guy tells his buddy that with women you need to use the Rule of Three: To find the truth, multiply by three the number of guys a woman says she's slept with. In the next scene a woman tells her friend that with guys you need to use the Rule of Three: To find the truth, divide by three the number of women a guy says he's slept with. Assume that each sex believes its own Rule of Three about the other sex, that guys seek to impress women with their prowess, and that women seek to impress guys with their demureness. What will each sex's strategy be, and what will the **equilibrium** be? Guys will claim as many women as is remotely credible; if they know women will divide by three, they should multiply the actual number by four. Women will claim as much demureness as is remotely credible; if they know guys will multiply by three, they should divide the actual number by four. The equilibrium will not be the truth or even three times (for men) and one-third (for women) of the truth. Instead, the sexes will go to opposite extremes, restrained only by the credibility of their claims. Rules of Three may be only a temporary equilibrium: If both sexes realize what's going on, each may develop a Rule of Four, a Rule of Five, or more.

> *Q: What if a woman announces that she is telling the truth? How will guys' strategies change?*

15.19

April 11, 2002—A story on Yahoo says that NBC is running a two-hour reunion special, *The Cosby Show: A Look Back*, on May 19, the final Sunday of the May ratings "sweeps" and the 2001–2002 television season. It will be one of the most competitive nights of network television in recent years. The showdown also has the series finale of Fox's *The X-Files* and the season enders of ABC's *The Practice* and CBS's *Survivor: Marquesas*. NBC's strategy in this **oligopoly** game is to be a bit different—to attract viewers who were hooked on the old *Cosby Show*. Some observers think that the total number of viewers that evening will rise because of NBC's offering—that this is a **positive-sum game**—and that the whole industry will benefit (perhaps at the expense of the cable networks). Others aren't so sure, with many believing that this is a **zero-sum game** and that NBC's offering will just take viewers away from the other three networks.

> *Q: If you were in charge of advertising for CBS and wanted to differentiate your product from those of Fox, ABC, and especially*

the new NBC entry, what kind of advertising slogans/arguments would you use (what would your advertising strategy be)?

15.20

Textbook publishers customarily send professors free "examination copies" of books they would like the professors to require their students to buy. A game theorist colleague has received an advertisement for a textbook on game theory. The publisher will send an examination copy if the professor returns a reply postcard and $3. Why the $3 charge? It's a trivial amount, not even enough to cover the **marginal cost** of printing and sending the book. The strategy is presumably designed to avoid sending books to professors who have no intention of assigning them in class. The publisher has defected from the **Nash equilibrium** of free copies for interested professors. My colleague has three strategies: forget it, instead send in the $3 with the postcard, or a third, clever strategy—send in the postcard with no money and punish the defector. He chose the third strategy. My guess is that other good game theorists will too. They will call the publisher's bluff. I expect the publisher will find that adding this charge doesn't work, and the game will revert to the Nash equilibrium of free copies to any interested professor.

> *Q: How would my colleague's strategy change if the charge had been $10? Would a different charge alter the Nash equilibrium?*

15.21

Data for 2001 show that over 1 percent of medical doctors in Arizona were severely punished by the state licensing board for grave deficiencies in their practices. This is four times higher than the rate in neighboring California. Does this mean that Arizona contains an unusual number of bad doctors? If federal **antitrust** authorities prosecute more proposed corporate takeovers, does that mean that there is a trend toward monopolization? More generally, if a regulatory or government agency finds more malfeasance in an industry, what does it mean? The answer is: Nothing. The rate of malfeasance that is discovered depends on both the extent of underlying problems and the regulatory agency's persistence in finding and punishing people and firms.

In considering differences in outcomes across states, where it is unlikely that underlying behavior differs very greatly, the role of government in searching for misbehavior is crucial. The same is true for variations over time in the extent of violations of federal regulations that are reported, because federal regulatory efforts vary greatly across presidential administrations.

> *Q: On your own campus what would you conclude about a report that incidents of cheating are most common in, for example, engineering classes? Are engineering students more likely to cheat?*

15.22

The federal government is seeking public comments on proposals that would allow airlines to impose surcharges on fares at peak business hours at the nation's busiest airports. Why don't the airlines just raise these fares themselves, since they are free to do so? The problem is that they often do try to raise fares, but without success. In the last two weeks two airlines have successively tried to increase discount fares by $20 per ticket, only to back down when they found that the other **oligopolists** did not follow their price increases. If the oligopolists can get the government to state that raising fares is justified as a way of reducing congestion at busy times and places, it is more likely that airlines generally will go along with price increases. A government statement would provide the "cover" industry members need to justify raising their prices at the same time; it would prevent competition between them.

> *Q: Is the government serving consumers' interests if it makes this kind of statement? If not, why would the government do such a thing?*

15.23

Another professor has caught a cheater. It's an open and shut case. If the professor files a formal charge with the university, however, she may be required to participate in a long judicial hearing. Her strategies are File the Charge and Don't File. If she does, the student faces universitywide disciplinary charges. The professor has given the student the choice of taking a course grade one level below what he otherwise would receive or facing a university hearing that could lead to his expulsion. Which choice—which strategy—will the student pick? Unless the student is a tremendous risk lover, he will choose to take the lower course grade and not risk expulsion. Taking the lower grade is his **dominant strategy.** The professor knew this when structuring the choices for the cheater, and she designed the choices to minimize the time she would have to spend on this case.

> *Q: Is this equilibrium **Pareto optimal**; that is, are both parties at least as well off as they would be in any other outcome of these strategies?*

15.24

Yale University is trying to get the federal government to allow it and other high-profile colleges and universities to collude to end their policy of early-decision admissions. Under this policy universities accept high school students in December of their senior year for entry the following September. This is a mechanism these elite schools use to compete for students. They don't like the outcome, and Yale and its colleagues are trying to end this policy. They argue that the universities admit early-decision students who are not as well qualified as some students whom they might admit at the regular decision time in April. Why is this different from any other group of **oligopolists** seeking government protection to create a **monopoly** and protect the group against its members' inability to collude successfully? Yale claims that early decision hurts the student. Yet whenever a "firm" states that it wants to collude with other firms to help customers, observers wonder how unselfish its motives really are.

> *Q: If you were defending Yale University in an **antitrust** case arising out of its collusive behavior, how would you justify Yale's behavior as benefiting the public as a whole?*

Tips on Hunting for Economics Everywhere in Part II

1. Look at how companies produce things and how you and your friends choose to do different activities. When the cost of producing changes, look at how the method of production changes.
2. Consider whether fixed costs are ignored in deciding on a course of action for the present and the future. Is a company—or are you—behaving in a maximizing way?
3. Consider how the price of a good is determined by costs and by ease of entry into the market. Think about why the price of a competitively produced good might differ across geographical areas.
4. Look for shocks to markets. They are always occurring, both naturally and because of government actions. How do they affect price and quantity? How do cost changes in particular affect price, quantity, and the number of suppliers?
5. Search for cases where people are dividing some fixed amount of anything. Can the group be made better off with a different division? If the amount changes, does the new distribution make everyone better off?
6. If there is only one supplier of a good or service, why? How is the monopoly protected? Does the monopolist account for the impact of raising price on the quantity he or she sells?
7. Look for monopolists charging different prices for the same good or service. Why are they doing it? How do they get away with it?
8. Look for suppliers colluding. Do they succeed? How do their strategies follow the ideas of game theory? Consider people's or countries' interactions in light of game theory.

PART III

Input Markets, the Public Sector, and International Markets

CHAPTER 16

Present Value and Discounting

16.1

A young economist told me of her recent trip to Guanajuato, Mexico. Land is scarce there, so burial in the local cemetery need not be permanent. The heirs have a choice of paying for ten, thirty, sixty, or ninety years or for permanent burial. Once the contract is paid, at the end of the specified time the deceased is dug up and cremated unless the lease is renewed. I wondered what the equilibrium price structure is. How much does the price rise as the length of time Grandpa is underground rises? The price should rise at a decreasing rate as the number of years rises, since *discounting* means that an extra year further in the future matters less, but one wonders whether people aren't willing to pay a big extra premium for knowing that Grandpa is buried safely for eternity. I would think that the price of keeping Grandpa underground for ninety years is less than three times as high as the thirty-year price but that the "forever" price exceeds the ninety-year price by a lot.

> *Q: Does a simple **discount rate,** say, 3 percent per year, apply here? If people put a high weight on knowing that Grandpa is buried for good, how would you describe the rate at which they implicitly discount years far out in the future compared to years in the nearer term?*

16.2

A running race is really an economic problem, analogous to the problem a country faces with a fixed nonrenewable resource, such as coal, that it wants to mine at an optimal rate over time. All runners have the problem of minimizing running time over the distance of a race. If they go out too fast, they poop out and wind up walking the last half of the race. If they conserve energy too much early in the race, they wind up with leftover strength near the end and are upset because they know they could have run the race faster. There is a correct rate at which to use one's physical reserves to get the best time, and it is related to the amount of resources, the depreciation rate, and the length of the **discounting period** (the race).

> *Q: Your rich uncle leaves you $10 million, and you know you can put it in the bank and get $500,000 in interest every year. Ask yourself: How much should I spend each year? (Remember, whatever you don't spend continues to get interest at 5 percent per year.)*

16.3

I have been running for exercise since 1967, in the early days averaging twenty-five miles a week, and these days twelve miles a week. Now my knees and hips hurt often. I always ran because I enjoyed it and thought it would be good for my long-term health. If I had known thirty-four years ago how much my lower body would hurt (and how likely it is that someday I will need knee and/or hip replacements), would I have run so much? Is our **forward-looking maximizing behavior** the same as the behavior we would have undertaken if we knew the long-term consequences of our activities? Do we **discount** the future at too high a rate when we are young?

> *Q: How does this vignette apply to your behavior in timing your studying for economics over the semester? Give examples of cases in which your behavior implies that you discount the future at a very high rate.*

16.4

My older son has a difficult business decision to make in his job as an internal consultant in a large banking corporation: The company can invest fairly cheaply in a set of software for its loan

officers. The new software will allow them to handle loan applications in a much more standardized way than before, and this
will save the company money. Alternatively, it can invest in a
more complex system that also will save money in the near
future but that will be more readily adaptable as future needs
change. He realizes that the choice depends in part on how the
company values the flexibility and savings in the future compared to the extra costs it must incur today. Today's very low
interest rates might tilt his decision toward investing in the more
complex software, since with a low interest rate the future gains
from the complex software should be valued more. He said that
the low interest rates also mean that the demand for loans today
is very high, so the company needs the software up and running
now to meet the demand.

> *Q: Say the simpler software saves $100,000 for each of the next
> ten years and the more complex software saves $150,000. The sim-
> ple software costs $500,000; the complex software costs $700,000.
> If the interest rate is zero, which choice should they make? What
> if the interest rate is 20 percent per year?*

16.5

Last night I went out to dinner at an excellent Mexican restaurant. I couldn't resist the frozen margarita, the enchiladas in mole
sauce, and the *crepas de cajeta*, crepes in a caramel type of sauce.
They taste so good, but I knew that I would not feel so great in
the morning. Sure enough, I was awake at 4:30 AM with an upset
stomach. As happens all too often, even though I know the consequences, when making the decision to eat I discounted those
future consequences so heavily that the current enjoyment more
than justified eating the good food. Regrettably, at 4:30 AM the
enjoyment had worn off, and I was bemoaning my high **discount
rate.**

> *Q: A similar example is a hangover, which should be fully
> expected if you drink too much. You know you'll get a hangover,
> and you keep drinking. What does that behavior, and the behavior
> in this vignette, tell you about your discount rate for the near
> future (the pleasure of tonight's drinking) versus the pain of
> tomorrow's hangover?*

16.6

My daughter-in-law has scheduled arthroscopic surgery on her knee. Surgery is an investment for her and in many other cases: There is no doubt that you are more debilitated after the surgery than you were before. Presumably you do it because eventually you'll be in better shape than you were before: The **present value** of the improvements exceeds the current cost. If you are quite old, the ailment is not too serious or restrictive, or the surgery is very invasive, it doesn't make sense to have it done. Even if the ailment isn't too serious and the surgery is very difficult, it could well make sense to do it if you are young and can envision many years of perfect health after the recovery period.

> *Q: What if the issue is not surgery but instead six months of very painful treatment for a cancer that currently is causing you no physical problems but that is potentially fatal (even though the chance of it being fatal is only 3 percent)? Would you take the treatment?*

16.7

February 8, 2002—I don't want to kick people when they are down, nor do I want to be nasty, but did the Enron employees who claim to have lost millions in retirement funds really lose that much? The appropriate way to think about their loss is not to compare the value of their Enron stock today (nearly zero) with what it was near its peak in January 2001 ($83 per share). Why should we feel sorry for them to the tune of what they would have had at the artificially inflated value of the stock at its peak? The appropriate measure of their loss is what the investment in their pensions (along with whatever Enron paid in for them) would have been worth if they had been receiving a normal rate of return from the time the money was invested. If, for example, someone put in $10,000 at the start of 1997, it would have risen to $43,000 by the end of 2000, but the loss is *not* $43,000. Instead, a reasonable measure of the loss, assuming a 10 percent rate of return over the four-year period, is $10,000*$[1.1]^4$ = $14,610, far smaller than the amount the Enron employees claim.

Q: What if the Enron employees argue, "But we had the $43,000, we had planned on having it for retirement, and now you're only giving us $14,610. We have lost."? How would you respond to that argument?

16.8

I buy a lottery ticket only when the jackpot exceeds $15 million. Each time I'm faced with a decision: Check off the "twenty-five equal annual payments" option or the "cash value" option. If the jackpot is $25 million and I check the first option, I get $1 million a year for twenty-five years if I win. I get about $14 million all at once (since the state uses an interest rate of about 5 percent for this purpose) if I check the cash value option. Which choice to make? (In terms of **present value** they're the same, since that is how the state obtains the cash value.) For me and for about 60 percent of the other ticket buyers, the choice is clear—take the cash value and run. It's better to have the money in my bank account now than to let the state dole it out to me. People choose the cash value option if they believe that they can invest it at a higher rate than the state can. They also choose it because their rate of impatience to spend the money is so great that they would rather have the chance of spending it now even if the amount to be spent is lower than it would be under the equal annual payments option.

Q: How should your choice of equal annual payments versus cash value be affected if the state of Texas suddenly figures the interest rate at 20 percent per year and discounts the cash value amount accordingly?

16.9

My eighty-six-year-old mother-in-law lives in Boston, 1,700 miles from us, and increasingly has trouble living on her own. My wife has to visit her a lot, and even then she needs more help from us. We could move her to Texas, but that would require a large burst of effort by my wife. Worse still, the move could take a large toll on my mother-in-law, especially as she has never lived outside the Boston area. Should we undertake this investment and the burdens it imposes on everyone or not? The decision should depend partly on how long we expect her to live, on the **discounting period.** If she were to move here and pass away next month, we would have incurred a large cost with very little gain in better care for her or more convenience for my wife. Worse, we would believe that the move shortened her life. However, if we knew that she would survive five more years, it would seem a worthwhile investment of time. In this case, as in any case with initial costs, knowing the length of the discounting period for an investment is crucial.

> *Q: How would the decision differ if my mother-in-law were seventy years old?*

16.10

Fixing Fluffy and Fido. The city of Houston gives a $15 discount on your pet license if the pet has been neutered. Ignoring whether you enjoy a neutered pet more or less than a natural one, is neutering a good investment? Say it costs $100 to have Fido neutered. This will yield a stream of savings of $15 per year as long as Fido lives. But the returns are in the future, and Fido isn't going to live forever. Even with a zero percent interest rate he has to live six and two-thirds years to make the investment worthwhile. If the interest rate is 5 percent, he has to live over eight years, and if it's 10 percent, he has to live eleven years. The city is offering an economic incentive, but it doesn't seem to be a very large one given the length of the **discounting period.**

> *Q: Using each of these interest rates, calculate how long the dog or cat has to live if the discount on the pet license is increased to $20 and the cost of neutering is $100.*

16.11

A (pretty bad) joke on the "Economist Joke" website (http://www.etla.fi/pkm/JokEc.html) goes, "I knew that economics was ruling my life when I tried to calculate my three-year-old son's **discount rate** by seeing how many sweets he would require to be promised to him after dinner to be equivalent to one sweet before dinner." Little kids discount the future at a very high rate. Let's say that the three-year-old is willing to give up one sweet before dinner in exchange for two sweets after dinner two hours later. That **trade-off** postpones gratification for one-twelfth of a day, or 1/4,380 of a year. The kid is insisting that his interest rate—the rate at which he discounts the future—is huge, far more than a trillion trillion percent per year. Kids are very impatient.

Q: Would the kid's implied interest rate be the same if the choice was $1 now or some amount of money after dinner? That is, would he insist on $2 after dinner, or might he settle for less after dinner?

CHAPTER 17

Wage Differences

17.1

September 29, 2001—How much is Michael Jordan worth to the Washington Wizards? I frankly doubt that he'll be anywhere near his former level of skill. (The guy's thirty-eight, and he hasn't played for three years.) But does this matter? His worth doesn't depend directly on how much he scores but on how much **revenue** is generated from ticket sales and TV because people want to see him. As long as his box-office luster doesn't wear off, his current points scored, rebounding, and so forth, don't matter too much.

> *Q: If Michael Jordan brings in an extra 5,000 fans per game, each paying $20 per ticket, and he plays fifty games, what is his* **marginal revenue product** *for the rest of this season?*

17.2

Government statistics show that in Texas beauticians earn $12.42 per hour, while barbers earn only $9.58, a ratio of 1.30. But in California, beauticians earn $9.96 per hour and barbers earn $8.74, a ratio of 1.14. Why is the relative wage of beauticians so much higher in Texas? Are the wage differentials caused by demand or supply forces? A sensible supply-side explanation is that being a beautician in Texas is harder work than being a beautician in California. Texas women are famous for "big hair," and generating big hair requires more effort and skill, and more time, than does giving an ordinary haircut of the kind that may be more common in California. Also, Texas men are more likely to have "buzz cuts" than are California surfer dudes. Since it's less difficult to give a buzz cut, the skills required of Texas barbers may be less than those required of California barbers. It's hard to think of a demand-side explanation that works this well. Even if demand for beauticians doing the same work that is done elsewhere were much higher in Texas, in the long run more workers in Texas would become beauticians than elsewhere. That would drive beauticians' wages back to the national equilibrium.

> *Q: If the wage of beauticians is so much higher in Texas, why don't California beauticians migrate to Texas and increase their wages by 25 percent?*

17.3

The Nakednews Channel, a Web-based service, presents news broadcasts, including foreign events, domestic events, business news, sports, and weather, by newscasters who are entirely naked. One wonders if the high pay of anchorpersons on the regular news channels isn't more for their looks than for their journalistic acumen. Nakednews takes this phenomenon one step further. What will happen to news anchors' pay if the naked phenomenon takes over television journalism entirely? Instead of merely having an ability to read the news well and look halfway decent from the shoulders up, news anchors also will need to look good fully unclothed. (This may present problems for Rather and Brokaw.) Fewer people will qualify to be network news anchors, and the **superstars** among tomorrow's naked anchors will receive even higher pay than is received by today's clothed news anchors.

> *Q: What would the widespread acceptance of Nakednews do to the relationship between wages and age in the television business?*

17.4

An economist has tabulated **revenue** from ticket sales at rock concerts in each of the last twenty years. Total ticket revenue has grown rapidly. The top 1 percent and top 5 percent of bands have received increasing shares of total revenue: There has been increasing inequality in band revenue. This has paralleled the growth in income inequality over this period. It may be due to the phenomenon of **superstars.** As concert venues get larger and more fans become familiar with the top groups through MTV and other sources that allow the biggest names to expand their markets, the top groups can reap sharply increased revenue. The lesser groups still have fans and do OK, explaining why total revenue in the industry has risen.

> *Q: What do you think will happen to inequality of rock bands' ticket sales if it becomes easier to download music from the Internet?*

17.5

My Ph.D. student has returned from a job visit to a private Eastern university. The number of economics majors at that school has skyrocketed, while the faculty has not been allowed to grow much. To generate a sufficient supply of sections of introductory economics the department chair has offered the department's Ph.D. students many opportunities to teach, with very good rates of pay (much higher than at most universities). Not surprisingly, a problem has arisen: The pay is so good that the students are happy to stay in school for many years and seem unwilling to complete their Ph.D. degrees. The chair thus faces an unpleasant **trade-off** in this labor market: Pay less and get lower-quality teaching or keep paying a lot and having a Ph.D. program in which students fail to complete the degree in a reasonable length of time.

> *Q: What would you do in the chair's position to ensure good teaching while encouraging the graduate students to finish their Ph.D. degrees?*

17.6

A nightclub pianist views his most dangerous job hazards as "Piano Man," "My Brown-Eyed Girl," and "American Pie." He hates playing them because he is asked to play them so often. He notes, however, that if a customer pays him $20, he'll play anything the customer wants, even these songs. **Compensating wage differentials** arise in employment but also in jobs that rely on tips. At some extra wage people will do a lot of things on the job that they would otherwise (for no or very little extra pay) find repugnant and refuse to do.

> *Q: If you work or have ever worked for pay, which things on your job do you find to be the most repugnant? How much pay per hour would you be willing to give up if you didn't have to do them?*

17.7

Legal and Liberal Minds at Work. The Texas Supreme Court now bars its law clerks—fresh law school graduates who have interned for a year at the court—from accepting the bonuses that private law firms typically pay their starting attorneys. Does this mean that their pay will be reduced? No way. All that will happen in this competitive labor market is that their annual pay will be slightly higher than it would have been, consistent with an amount needed to compensate them for the time they spent as clerks and the prestige value of having them on the law firm's staff. Whether the compensation comes in an initial bonus or as extra annual pay is irrelevant; the market for young lawyers' services is competitive and will cause the net pay to remain unchanged. The chief justice of the Court recognized the role of economics by noting that the ethics rules don't prevent young lawyers from receiving higher salaries as a result of the experience gained during their clerkships.

> *Q: What would happen to pay in the market for professional football players if the NCAA prohibited professional teams from offering signing bonuses to college players during the NFL draft?*

17.8

An economics professor at another university has obtained offers to change schools from three other high-prestige institutions. He clearly has been out soliciting offers and has created a bidding war for his services. He is a good economist but certainly no **superstar.** Other people who are as good as or better than he, as economists seem unable to generate this kind of competition for their services (and unable to get their salary bid up in the way he is doing). Why this guy? He has one thing going for him: His spouse does not work in the labor market. Everybody knows this, and everybody knows that his costs of moving to a different location are lower than those of people with working spouses. This means that any other university that offers him a job need not fear that he is stuck where he is. They believe that they have a good chance of attracting him. General awareness of his mobility increases the threats he can bring to bear on his current employer. He may not in fact leave his current school, but whether he does or doesn't, his potential mobility helps raise his earning power.

> *Q:* *If this guy's wife worked in the labor market and earned a lot of money, would he be able to get these universities to bid for his services? What if his wife worked but earned the* **minimum wage?**

17.9

A professor of French literature was complaining about the high salaries paid to economics professors at this university and other universities. He is a competent researcher and teacher, has a Ph.D., and has twenty years of experience, yet he makes less than the new Ph.D. graduates we are hiring to start their teaching and research careers. He viewed this difference as absurd. Why should he with his skills be paid less? His job is no more fun than mine; he's not giving up any pay because he enjoys his work much more than economics professors enjoy theirs. He's paid less because of **supply** and **demand** in a competitive labor market. A lot of people want to be French professors relative to universities' demand for them, and relatively few want to be economics professors compared to the demand for them. The difference arises because there are many jobs outside college teaching for economists and people who might become economists. To maintain an economics faculty, universities have to compete for talent. There are few alternative employment opportunities for would-be French professors. This is sad because we're really doing the same job. But if a university went ahead and paid equally, lowering economists' pay and raising French professors' pay, it would have a great French faculty and a dreadful bunch of economists. No competent economist would want to come to such a university, and the ones already there would soon leave for greener pastures.

> *Q: If you were a university president and wanted to maintain the quality of the faculty in all your fields without having a large budget, what, if anything, could you do to satisfy the French professor in this example?*

17.10

The song "Proud Mary" by Creedence Clearwater Revival begins, "Left a good job in the city, workin' for the Man every night and day." This is a really silly sentence. If the person was working "every night and day," it couldn't have been "a good job." That implies many hours of work each week. In the United States only a small fraction of workers put in more than fifty hours per week, many of them self-employed professionals and highly paid managers, not the kind of person who might be singing this song. Also, if the person worked at night, it is unlikely that the job was good: Nighttime work is most common among workers with few skills and low wages. It is also more prevalent among workers in minority groups that are discriminated against. Night work pays better than comparable day work—there is a **compensating wage differential** for night work—but not much better. Work at night is typically undesirable work.

> *Q: Find a want ad for a nighttime job. Look at the wage being offered and compare it to a want ad for a similar job with a daytime schedule.*

17.11

March 25, 2002—Ryan O'Neal and Ali MacGraw, two stars of the late 1960s, presented an Oscar last night. They looked really old. With Hollywood's and America's fascination with youth, it's not surprising that you don't see them on the screen anymore. For most movie stars the peak comes by age forty. This is early, but the careers are long compared to those of star professional football and basketball players. With careers that short, their annual earnings have to be high enough in their few good years to com-

pensate for the many years of normal earnings that they might
have gotten in most other occupations, where you don't reach
peak earnings until age fifty or even the mid-fifties. Short careers
don't account for most of the immense earnings of movie stars
and professional sports heroes, but they do explain part of those
earnings.

*Q: Suddenly old becomes beautiful. What will happen to the
earnings of younger movie actors as a result?*

17.12

The life of a clergyperson—minister, rabbi, or whatever—seems
very difficult. It's not the sermonizing or leading religious services but rather the need to minister to families at times of grave
personal stress: divorce, serious illness, or death. You would
think that it would take a high wage—a large **compensating
wage differential**—to draw people into the profession. In fact, if
you adjust for everything that you might think affects earnings—
education, age, location, race, sex, ethnicity, hours of work, and
so on—male clergy in the United States earn less than 60 percent
of what otherwise identical workers earn. Why? It has to be that
there are enough people who enjoy helping other people at difficult times and are willing to work in a very low-paid occupation.
Without that kind of willingness for self-sacrifice—without people who have a "calling" to the ministry—we would quickly be
unable to attract enough people into this occupation to fill all the
pulpits in a religious country like the United States.

*Q: What would happen to the wage of clergy, compared to other
college graduates, if the government launched an advertising campaign to get more people to become ministers, rabbis, and priests?*

17.13

Economists in the United States and elsewhere have studied the
wages of gay and lesbian workers in comparison to those of other
workers. One study deals with the Netherlands. The research
shows that after adjusting for things such as age, education, location, and other determinants of wages, gay male workers earn at
least 3 percent less than do otherwise identical men. Lesbians earn

at least 3 percent more than do otherwise identical women. Previous studies for the United States tell a similar story. Do these pay differences reflect **discrimination** in favor of lesbians and against gays? Perhaps there is generalized discrimination in favor of "maleness," and stereotypical male traits are rewarded whether they are exhibited by men or by women. Lesbians earning more than other women may just reflect a broader kind of discrimination based on traits rather than gender.

> *Q: Given the results reported in this vignette, how do you think the earnings of bisexual men would differ from those of heterosexual men? Those of bisexual women from those of heterosexual women?*

17.14

Mary Chapin Carpenter's song "He Thinks He'll Keep Her" tells of a woman who has three children in quick succession, stays home to take care of them, and then gets divorced at age thirty-six. Thereafter, "For fifteen years she had a job and not one raise in pay, now she's in the typing pool at **minimum wage.**" I doubt that she had no raise in pay for fifteen years. But that she didn't earn very much is not surprising. During the time of life when most people are investing in **human capital** on the job, she stayed home. Her marketable skills didn't grow, and whatever skills she had before she got married depreciated. Wage growth represents a return to investment in human capital, and the skills learned on the job represent a large part of every worker's human capital.

> *Q: If you don't plan to start working until age thirty-five, what kinds of occupations should you train for? What college majors would be appealing?*

17.15

Jack Benny was a famous radio and television comedian in the 1930s through 1950s, most noted for being incredibly stingy. A robber accosted him and snarled, "Your money or your life!" Benny stood silent for several minutes, and the robber asked him what was taking so long. Benny said, "I'm thinking about it, I'm thinking about it!" Most people wouldn't ponder this **trade-off** for long. While we typically don't buy our lives with money, we implicitly do make these choices every time we take a job or pay for medical care. Evidence from labor markets and the medical care industry shows that people are willing to pay $30,000 to $50,000 to reduce their risk of death in a year by 1 percent. Extrapolating to a 100 percent risk of dying (certain death), this implies that people value their lives at $3 million to $5 million. These values far exceed the **present value** of the earnings of the typical American (who averages $40,000 per year for each of forty years in the labor market).

> *Q: How much would you pay (at age twenty) for a guarantee that instead of living to eighty, you would live to eighty-one? How much do you think a healthy person who is eighty-five would be willing to pay for a guarantee of living to age ninety-one instead of ninety?*

17.16

The CEO of a major company was commenting that his staff had found that undergraduate major and GPA had no impact on a worker's success in the company. If the CEO believes the study, I hope he follows a new hiring policy: The company should hire new employees who majored in subjects whose graduates generally aren't paid well. He also should hire only those with C averages. There are positive wage differentials for good grades and for harder majors. Among graduates of the University of Texas, within the same major an A-minus student makes about 8 percent more than does a B-minus student by age thirty-five. If, for example, the company hired College of Education graduates with low grades, the CEO would be hiring inexpensive labor. If he believes they are just as productive as anyone else, he should do so. Deep down, though, he probably doesn't believe his company's study.

> *Q: What if the market discriminates against a group of workers who are just as productive as other, more highly paid workers? As a smart manager, what kind of workers should you hire?*

CHAPTER 18

Labor Market Behavior and Poverty

18.1

The state of Texas is starting up a new set of certifications of legal specialties. My wife faces the choice of whether to sign up to take the test and become board-certified in her legal specialty. This is a difficult decision: She plans to practice only for seven or eight more years, not a very long time for the gains from being board-certified to outweigh the cost of time spent studying for and agonizing about the results of the test. If other, younger lawyers become board-certified, however, she will look like a second-rate lawyer. She won't have the certification and might lose clients to certified lawyers or have trouble attracting new clients. The optimal amount to invest in **human capital** depends on your age but also on the choices made by your competitors in the labor market.

> *Q: How would my wife's decision differ if she were age sixty-three? What choice should she make if at age sixty-three the state requires her to become board-certified if she is to continue in legal practice? What factors would affect her decision?*

18.2

Listening to Mick Jagger sing "Satisfaction" today reminded me of my favorite example of **economic rent:** two guys, each fifty-nine years old, each having majored in economics in college, each running long-distance for exercise, and each having a child who graduated from Yale. The two guys are Mick Jagger and I. We probably have the same **opportunity cost:** For both of us the alternative uses of our time aren't great. Both of us earn more than our opportunity cost, but Mick earns much more than I do, so he is receiving much more economic rent than I am. The British or American government could tax Mick's music earnings a lot, and he would still be willing to continue singing. If they imposed a huge tax on my earnings from economics, they'd be taxing away more than my economic rent, and I'd quit teaching economics.

> *Q: Let's say I earn $100,000 as an economist and my next-best alternative is as a singer earning $20,000. How much could the government tax away without me leaving economics to become a singer?*

18.3

A local "think tank" reported on its new study "showing" that it takes at least $44,000 for a family of four to enjoy the basic necessities in central Texas. Since we had just talked in class about the poverty threshold for a family of four in the United States being $18,000, one wonders what this group means by "basic necessities." By broadening the definition of poverty so greatly, this kind of exaggeration diminishes our concern for people who are truly poor and for whom we do need to design policies. If half the population is defined as poor, those who really are poor will not be given the help they need.

> *Q: What are your "basic necessities"? Do you believe that the American taxpayer should be required to guarantee that you can purchase these necessities?*

18.4

Because my undergraduate econometrics class has sixty students, I do not have the time to deal with each student in developing the short term paper that I require. Instead I am asking students to work in pairs. The **matching** of students to form these pairs is an interesting example of two-sided matching, something that economists have studied in a variety of entry-level job markets. If all that matters is getting the best grade on the term paper with the minimum of effort, each student will want to match with the best student (in terms of both ability and willingness to work) in the class. If the best student is already matched, the remaining students presumably will want to match with the next-best student, and so on. If there is perfect information about each student's ability, the equilibrium will be the optimal one for eliciting performance: The top student will match with the next-best, students 3 and 4 will match, and so on. Unfortunately, information is far from perfect, and factors other than expected performance may enter into matching decisions. Regrettably, I expect to have a number of pairs where one student winds up doing almost all the work.

> *Q: How is the matching process described here affected if I allow some students to write a paper alone (without any co-worker)? Now consider matching in the market for spouses. How does the two-sided matching in that market resemble that in the "market" for paper coauthors? What is the equivalent in the marriage market of a student writing a paper alone? How does it affect the equilibrium matching in that market?*

18.5

January 25, 2002—A headline in yesterday's *New York Times* read, "Many ride out the recession in a graduate school harbor." The story goes on to talk about a sharp rise in enrollments "in schools of business, law, journalism, education and many other graduate programs as laid-off workers and college seniors are deciding to wait out the recession." A recession is a good time to obtain additional education. The tuition is no lower, but the **opportunity cost** of the student's time is low in a recession because the student would have a hard time finding a job. The rise in enrollments in recessions, even though incomes may fall, suggests that the opportunity cost of schooling is a major determinant of graduate enrollment in the United States and is far more important than the direct cost in dollars.

> *Q: Have tuition increases affected your decision about where and when to attend college or university? If they have, why might the answer be different for decisions about going to college compared with going to graduate school?*

18.6

If you ever attend a play or concert, you notice that the lines for women's rest rooms are almost always longer than those for men's rest rooms. This is no doubt a result of basic biological and cultural differences that guarantee that with the same number of usable toilets, women's waits will be longer. The question is whether this is fair: Are facilities discriminating when they contain rest rooms that guarantee that women will have to wait longer? A number of states have responding by enacting "toilet **equity**" laws, requiring in some cases that the average waiting times be equal (which requires more women's than men's toilets). Whether these laws make sense depends on whether you believe that no **discrimination** means equality of access or equality of outcomes. The issue thus mirrors the general question of discrimination in education, labor markets, and other areas. Is it opportunity or outcomes that should concern us? In this case, do we mean access in terms of number or access in terms of time spent?

> *Q:* *How do you respond to the argument that it makes sense for women to wait in bathroom lines longer, since the average women's time is less valuable than the average man's if we measure the value of time by market wages?*

18.7

February 12, 2002—An ad during the winter Olympics showed a family with a one-year-old child, with the parents saying that he always liked to jump. It shows the same kid at ages three, seven, and ten and then shows him winning the 1998 ski jump event and his parents saying how much effort they put into encouraging him and how much time they devoted to his training. This ad illustrates the role of investment in training of any kind in generating success. It makes it abundantly clear that excellence in any activity depends only partly on inherent ability and inclinations. Being top-notch in a field requires ability, but it also requires a very large investment of one's own time and that of one's instructors.

> *Q:* *Compare a champion marathon runner and a champion baseball player. Describe the nature of the investments in training that*

each must make and consider whether raw ability is relatively more
or less important in marathon running or in playing baseball.

18.8

February 13, 2002—Derek Parra, the American ice skater who won an Olympic silver medal this week, grew up in southern California, not the usual locale for ice-skating champions. Parra was a champion in-line skater who wanted to go to the Olympics but couldn't because in-line skating is not an Olympic event. He was persuaded to try ice skating, and his skills were readily transferable to this more established sport. If in-line skating did not exist, Parra would not be an Olympic ice skater. This is a case in which technological change (the development of in-line skating, which did not occur until the 1980s) enabled a wide range of people to develop skills that are easily transferred to a different activity (ice skating). How many other new technologies (perhaps video games) have enabled people to develop skills that enhance their productivity in older, more established activities?

Q: Give other examples of these kinds of complementary skills.
For example, how might skills honed playing pool be transferable
to one's activity as a batter in baseball?

18.9

Until 1975 the federal National Institutes of Health (NIH) identified young scientists and offered them careerlong financial support (salary only) to do research at their own university laboratories. Only ten such grants were in force at any time. The NIH discovered that about half the scientists continued to do good research over most of their lifetimes, while the other half soon stopped doing serious research and happily enjoyed their sinecures. To someone who thinks economic considerations dominate everything, the surprising fact is that half the scientists continued to work productively. Financial incentives do matter, and no doubt that is why the NIH abolished the program and replaced it with five-year renewable grants. But nonfinancial incentives—the desire to excel, the desire to avoid embarrassment, and the love of one's work—provide an important spur too. For people who are motivated by these incentives the financial rewards are at least partly **economic rent** to an activity they would pursue even at lower pay.

> *Q: Michael Jordan made $40 million per year playing basketball and endorsing products. If the government taxed away $35 million, would Michael still have played basketball and done product endorsements? How much of his $40 million earnings is economic rent?*

18.10

My wife thinks this book will be a tremendous success. She's concerned about the contract I will be receiving from the publisher and asks, "What if the book is really successful and they try to exploit you with a lousy contract on a subsequent edition?" I tell her that they might try to do that, but if they do, I can always threaten to walk away and redo the book for another publisher. Both the publisher and I hold some power over each other in this case—it is a **bilateral monopoly.** The distribution of the gains from any success the book has depends on my ability to bargain well with the publisher. From past observation my wife believes that I have no ability to bargain with anybody over anything; she believes that I will always wind up being exploited. In economic terms, she is convinced that the publisher will extract all the **economic rent** from the book's success, leaving me with no more than a competitive rate of return on my effort.

> *Q: How would my wife's concerns differ if she felt that there were lots of equally good competitors for this volume? How concerned should she be about my inability to bargain well?*

18.11

Some distinguished pop musicians, including Eagles' former lead singer Don Henley, are lobbying to outlaw long-term contracts between recording companies and young artists, arguing, "We're expected to indefinitely fund the record company" (*The Wall Street Journal*). I worry about the results of limiting people's freedom to contract. Without long-term contracts no record company will bear the costs of developing a singer's potential. If it bore those costs and the singer was soon free to contract with a different recording label, the first company would lose its entire investment in the young singer's **human capital** when the singer left. Knowing that, companies wouldn't enter into such contracts, and many singers wouldn't break into the business unless they found some other source for the initial costs of setting up their acts. Henley argues that the record companies are using profits from his records to subsidize bad singers. They are using those profits to subsidize the training of new singers. They may be investing unwisely, but it is hard to argue that they are purposely choosing to subsidize losers. The company presumably takes risks, and some don't pan out. They would not be the first companies to invest unwisely.

Q: In the market for football players, how are potential stars trained, and who pays the costs?

18.12

Is it better to hire someone who will do barely enough with certainty or someone who might be great or might be a disaster? Do we really choose to hire those potential employees whose expected **marginal revenue product** is above their wage rate? If we can hire as many workers as we want, that textbook approach is correct. But what if you are limited in the number you can hire? And what if you can fire the workers who turn out to be duds, which is true in most nonunion workplaces in the United States? In that case it pays to look not only at the amount that you expect the worker to produce but also at the maximum that she or he might generate for the company. This is evident in hiring new faculty members. We can always deny lifetime tenure to those who turn out to be mediocre; we can fire them after a probationary period of six years. And we gain prestige from those who end up doing really important research. With that reward structure in universities it pays to choose a riskier faculty member—one who might bomb or who might produce Nobel Prize–winning research— over a competent plodder who offers no risks. The same considerations apply in any business where individual productivity matters a lot and where the company chooses between two workers it expects to be equally productive on average.

Q: What would happen in this situation if the government passed a law requiring universities to grant tenure or fire the faculty after a shorter probationary period, say, only three years? How should our decision change?

18.13

March 8, 2002—Congress is about to pass a law that would extend unemployment benefits from twenty-six to thirty-nine weeks in many states as long as the United States stays in recession. Similar laws have been passed in every recession since 1958. There is a real **trade-off** here. Making the benefits last longer helps maintain the spending of the unemployed, but the longer benefits give unemployed workers an incentive to stay unemployed. This is true whether we're in a recession or not. The argument for extension is that in a recession, the balance tilts more toward helping the unemployed because the incentive to remain unemployed matters little if few jobs are available. There's good statistical evidence that the disincentive to work generated by unemployment benefits is much smaller in recessions. Well and good, but the problem has always been how to turn off the spigot of unemployment benefits soon enough when the economy recovers to prevent them from making unemployment too attractive an option for people who would otherwise easily find jobs.

Q: If there are few jobs available in the recession, why not allow people to draw unemployment benefits for fifty-two weeks? Or sixty-five weeks? Or until they find a job?

18.14

Recent news reports say companies are abolishing or limiting "casual day," typically a Friday when workers are allowed and even encouraged to come to the office in casual instead of business attire. Does this represent a sudden change in attitudes about what is appropriate? Maybe, but it could just reflect a change in how tight the labor market is. Casual days may have been needed to provide employees with **incentives** not to quit and attract new employees when jobs were extremely plentiful. (The late 1990s saw the lowest unemployment rates in thirty years.) Casual days were a way of compensating employees without raising pay. With a recession and fewer available jobs, this form of compensation is no longer as necessary. The downfall of casual days also suggests that employers did not view them as a way of increasing productivity: If casual days raised productivity, employers would be even more interested in having workers dress casually now, when concerns about keeping productivity high are even greater than they are during a boom.

> *Q: In the late 1990s there were many newspaper stories about companies offering their employees on-site health clubs. How would a recession affect the number of companies providing that fringe benefit?*

18.15

A woman weighing 240 pounds conducts an aerobics class in San Francisco. The woman had been denied a job by a for-profit fitness center. She sued under San Francisco law, which prohibits **discrimination** based on appearance, arguing that she had been leading aerobics classes for fifteen years. Was she being discriminated against because of her weight? In other words, was this pure discrimination? Or was she not hired because her potential employer felt that her weight would ensure that few or no clients would take her classes? Was this a sound commercial decision based on her likely productivity? It is impossible to decide between these two possibilities, and this is true generally in cases where the source of potential bias is consumer preferences. The same arguments can be made about discrimination against minorities or women: Businesspeople could always rationalize a refusal to hire on grounds that hiring would be bad for business. If determining the underlying cause is so difficult, in the end we have to decide which groups to protect on political, not economic, grounds.

> *Q: Give arguments in favor of protecting the overweight against discrimination of this kind. Then give arguments against protecting them.*

18.16

At the urging of many citizens and members of the legislature, my university is considering abandoning or minimizing its use of SAT scores in admissions. The University of California has already greatly reduced its use of test scores. Is this a good idea? At my university, a study of a large random sample of graduates shows that within the same major and separately by gender, and adjusting for how well students performed in high school, those with higher SAT scores when they applied had higher GPAs at graduation from the university. Each extra 100 SAT points adds 0.12 extra GPA points. For example, going from 1,100 to 1,200 raises GPA from 3.00 to 3.12. SAT shouldn't be the sole criterion for admission, but the fact that it offers independent evidence on how well a student will perform in college means that the information it provides should not be entirely ignored, since it indicates how productive investments in **human capital** might be.

> *Q: If instead of abandoning SAT scores in admission the university decides to stop using high school rank, would the kinds of students—race, sex, and so on—admitted to the university be any different? If you must abandon SAT or high school rank, which one should be dropped?*

18.17

The guy in the airplane seat next to me says he was fired from his job as a marketing vice president when his company was taken over by a European conglomerate. The new owner, like all employers contemplating firing long-term workers, did not want to indicate that the man's job was in jeopardy. If it had done so, the man might have quit while the company still wanted his services. A number of studies have shown that workers are generally surprised by plant closings and mass layoffs: Companies successfully hide information about impending firings. This man, though, had an inkling that his job was in trouble: Instead of printing up two boxes of business cards, the new company gave him only ten cards, and the cards didn't even have his job title printed on them.

> *Q: Why would a business not want to tell a worker that his or her job will end in one month? Why isn't the company better off*

if he or she quits now and the company avoids paying unemploy-
ment benefits and severance pay?

18.18

We were talking about the news that Iran may be paying $25,000
to the families of suicide bombers. A colleague remarked that this
is probably the entire present value of their lifetime earnings: the
value of their **human capital.** This is reminiscent of a calculation
an economist did in the early 1960s. After the Bay of Pigs debacle—the failed attempt to take over Cuba in 1961, shortly after
Fidel Castro had assumed power—the prisoners Castro had cap-
tured were exchanged for tractors and medicine. The economist
showed that the market price of this material, $53 million, was
very close to the value of the 1,113 prisoners' human capital—the
discounted value of their lifetime earnings. Castro, by now one of
the last communist leaders, had a good intuitive grasp of market
economics early in his career.

> *Q: What would happen to the amount Castro was paid if the
> prisoners were all men age sixty?*

18.19

April 11, 2002—Arlette Laguiller, a far-left candidate in the
upcoming French presidential election, promises to push for a
law banning layoffs in France. Who could object to this? Layoffs
hurt workers and their families. But this law has other effects too.
If employers can never lay off a worker, they know they will be
stuck with unproductive workers when the demand for their
products drops. To prevent this—and the likelihood of large
losses in bad times—companies will be less likely to hire workers during good times. Instead, they will rely on a smaller work-
force, just enough employees to keep a company profitable during bad times. They will have these few people work more
overtime hours during good times. Madame Laguiller's idea will
stop layoffs and reduce employment fluctuations. It will also
reduce employment—the number of jobs in the economy.

> *Q: This legislation creates a **trade-off:** more jobs or more secu-
> rity for fewer workers. Which side of the trade-off do you prefer?*

18.20

There were two choices for an assisted-living facility (all meals provided along with some personal services) for my mother-in-law. The less expensive one has bigger apartments, is three years newer, and has a better location than the more expensive one. We chose the more expensive one. The reason is that the marketing person at the physically nicer one admitted that they regularly lose employees to the one we have chosen. We've also heard from friends that the staff at the place we chose is extremely gentle and caring toward the residents. The reason it is more expensive is that it pays its workers more. The higher wages attract a higher-quality staff, but the costs have to be passed on to the consumer in this competitive market.

> *Q: Look at the part-time jobs your fellow students have. Is there a relationship between how much they earn and your perception of their potential quality as employees?*

18.21

The comedy group the Kids in the Hall claimed, "The only thing worse than not having a job is looking for one." Searching for a job is unpleasant, but it can't be worse than not having a job. If it were worse, if the **marginal cost** of searching for even one hour exceeded the marginal benefit from finding a job, no one would search. Since you have to search to find a job, if the Kids were correct, nobody would search and nobody would have a job. The fact that most people have jobs provides evidence that for most people the marginal cost of at least some hours of job search is less than the **marginal benefit.**

> *Q: If searching for work is unpleasant, why doesn't the government subsidize it to reduce the burden? What would happen to unemployment if there were such* **subsidies***?*

18.22

A report on CNN states, "Ten years ago only 16 percent of the highest-income families borrowed for college. By 2000 that had grown to 45 percent." This should not be surprising, and it doesn't indicate that today's higher-income families are poverty-stricken. It's a rational response to changing costs and benefits. The costs of borrowing to finance a college education are fairly low today because interest rates are far below what they were in the 1980s. The returns of going to college—the return on the investment in **human capital** that is represented by time in college and a college degree—far exceed the costs of borrowing. It makes sense to borrow when the returns exceed the costs, and that's just what students are doing. Students are doing exactly the right thing given the incentives the market is providing.

> *Q: If you did not take out student loans, why not? If you did, could you have borrowed more? If yes, why didn't you borrow more?*

18.23

People engage in job searches; they also search for spouses through dating and other activities. They will search more if the dispersion of the outcomes they might obtain (the quality of the jobs or the quality of the marriage partners) is greater. In the last three decades there has been a tremendous decline in marriage rates in the United States. Over this time period inequality of earnings among men has risen sharply. It pays a woman who is searching in the marriage market to postpone marriage when inequality among men is greater, because the benefits from waiting longer to find "Mr. Right" are greater when he differs more from the average guy the woman might find. Two economists have shown that the age at which women marry has risen most rapidly in cities where inequality among men's earnings has risen the most. Rational search described changes in American women's marriage patterns in the late twentieth century, and it probably still does. This isn't the only cause of later marriages: Better job opportunities for women matter a lot, but changing incentives to search in the marriage market have led women to postpone marriage.

> *Q: African-American men's earnings inequality has risen more than has that of whites. What do you think has happened to the marriage rate among African-American women?*

18.24

Employers in many continental European countries offer much more job security to employees than their U.S. counterparts do. To overcome the inflexibility this creates, they also have vast numbers of employees on so-called fixed-term contracts, jobs that have a limited duration. These jobs are increasingly widespread; in Spain, for example, they now account for over 20 percent of employees. A new study shows that there is a downside to these contracts: In Spain such workers have substantially higher accident rates than do otherwise identical workers on permanent contracts, even newly hired permanent workers. Workers on fixed-term contracts don't expect to remain in the firm very long. With a short expected tenure, they have no incentive to invest in **human capital** in the form of the time and effort to learn safer methods of production. They also have incentives to cut corners in the hopes of demonstrating to the employer that they are productive enough to be one of the very few (currently roughly 5 percent) fixed-contract employees who obtain a permanent job. Their higher accident rates are the unsurprising result of this combination of incentives.

Q: In light of this argument, what do you expect will happen to job accidents in a recession, when hiring is reduced?

CHAPTER 19

Externalities, Public Goods, and Property Rights

19.1

November 19, 2001—At the Atlanta airport last Friday one individual tried to save himself a bit of time by avoiding the security lines. His efforts, which in the short run made him better off, caused huge **negative externalities,** as the airport was closed for three hours and air traffic in the Southeast was severely disrupted. One wonders whether the guy has sufficient funds to compensate society for the costs he imposed.

> *Q: How would you measure the costs this clown imposed on the rest of society? What do those costs consist of? Having calculated those costs, would you set the penalty on him equal to that amount, higher, or lower?*

19.2

One of the teaching assistants pointed out a neat **free-rider** problem. A friend of hers was getting married. That was one of a number of weddings that took place in the church over a weekend. There was no time to put in new flowers before each wedding, so the brides were asked to chip in for the flowers. Several brides said no; those who said yes paid for the flowers (presumably the private benefit to each was large enough to exceed the flowers' cost), and the flowers were installed. The other brides paid nothing but had the **free-rider** benefit of the flowers.

Q: *What could the individual brides have done to get the others to pay a "fair share" of the costs of the flowers? Is there any way the free-rider brides could have been compelled to pay?*

19.3

A recent news story showed how complex the interactions that involve **externalities** can be. There has been overfishing of pollock in Alaskan waters. This has, so scientists claim, reduced the population of seals, which eat pollock. With fewer seals, orca whales have lost their favorite prey and have had to move closer to shore to prey on sea otters. The sea otter population is down, allowing their prey—sea urchins—to multiply rapidly and chew up the underwater kelp forests near the shore. Since the kelp forests aren't there, the shorelines are more exposed to waves that generate beach erosion and have caused an increasing loss of shoreline housing. (This chain is sort of like the children's verse "The House That Jack Built.") This six-step externality is the most complex I've heard of. It illustrates how something seemingly harmless—overfishing just one species—can generate serious negative effects in an area that to a layperson would seem very far removed from the action that originally produced the externality.

Q: *List three remedies that the government could introduce to reduce the problem of beach erosion presented in this vignette. Discuss the total social costs presented by each of your solutions.*

19.4

A headline states, "Catalytic converter helps stop potential suicides." Catalytic converters are placed on automobiles to meet antipollution requirements. To overcome the **negative externalities** generated by pollution, car owners pay higher prices that reflect the cost of these mandated devices. The converters reduce the amount of harmful gases cars generate, including carbon monoxide. The story tells of a man who locked himself in his garage with the car running. After ten hours he was conscious and still breathing. If he had tried this before the mid-1980s, without the converter, he would have been dead in thirty minutes. The reduction of one negative externality led to seemingly unrelated consequences that most people would view as beneficial.

Q: Let's say that new cheaper antipollution devices are created that replace the catalytic converter but don't reduce carbon monoxide as much. Would you favor allowing the use of these new devices? Why or why not?

19.5

The new personal transporter, which looks like a cross between a lawn mower and a Razor scooter, was unveiled. Should I buy one? This seems to be a serious **externalities** issue: Do I want to be driving one down the street at seventeen miles per hour (mph) while other folks are whizzing by me in their two-ton SUVs at fifty mph? That sounds like a recipe for death. Until enough others are driving them, I don't want to be on the streets with one. I don't want to be the one to bear the costs of the **negative externalities** imposed by drivers of large vehicles.

Q: What does the viewpoint expressed here say about the desirability of buying a small sports car such as a Miata?

19.6

There was a huge accident on the interstate early this morning, when a large truck overturned. It took five hours to clear up, and people said their commuting time in many cases was increased by an hour. As often happens, the truck was improperly loaded and/or the guy took a turn too fast. The cost of the accident is staggering. There is only minor damage to the truck, but the main thing is the time lost—perhaps 20,000 people, each spending an extra hour in traffic, each of whose time averages $15 at least—a total of at least $300,000. You also have to add in the cost of wreckers, police, and so forth. Why can't fines to derelict truckers reflect the full cost of the accidents they generate, the **negative externalities** produced by those accidents? That should substantially reduce incentives for improper loading and bad driving.

*Q: In many cases this kind of regulation is made impossible by the **transaction costs** of assessing damages and imposing fines. What are these transaction costs? Be specific. Is there any way to assess fines and penalties without incurring these costs?*

19.7

Fight at the Health Club Illustrates Transaction Costs. The Health Club limits the use of elliptical trainers to thirty minutes, and you cannot reserve them ahead of time. There are two women who sign up for elliptical trainers at the health club and then wait five minutes to get on them. They also reserve the ellipticals for forty-five minutes. Both of these practices violate the rules. Today my wife got on the "reserved" machine and got into an argument with one of the women. The person running the Club said it's OK for someone to sign-up for forty-five minutes if no one is waiting (even though signs say it's against the rules) so long as he or she gets off when asked by a person who is waiting. This imposes **transaction costs** on the person waiting rather than on the violator who claimed **property rights** on the machine by hogging it for forty-five minutes. **Transaction costs** matter a lot.

> *Q: How can the Health Club make the person who is imposing the **negative externality**—hogging the machines—bear the costs of the **externality** generated by her bad behavior?*

19.8

In my office hours I mentioned to a student that I pay my teaching assistants $5 each if someone gets 90 percent or more correct on the final exam. I had previously paid off only twice in twenty-nine years of teaching large introductory sections (total enrollment about 15,000 students over the years). The student pointed out very cleverly that any student who does well creates a **positive externality** (the dollars paid to the TAs), so students in the class should be subsidized to give them proper incentives to study hard. In fact, one student (the boyfriend of the woman who pointed this out) did get over 90 percent (sixty-seven correct out of seventy-two questions) even without the incentive. Think how many more students might have done this well with an incentive.

> *Q: Who should offer the subsidy, the teaching assistants or me?*

19.9

We awoke in the middle of the night and smelled skunk odor all over the house. I called the pest control company, and the guy came out to the house. He went under the house and showed us where he thought the skunk was living. He said that the best way to get rid of the skunk is to leave a bright light shining and a radio blaring overnight. (I call this the Manuel Noriega approach to animal removal, after the Panamanian president who was removed from office by the U.S. military and subjected to this treatment.) After a day the hungry and thirsty skunk will run away and make his den elsewhere in the neighborhood. I apply the treatment, although I'm aware that I am creating a **negative externality** in the neighborhood: One of my lucky neighbors no doubt will find that the skunk has taken up residence under his or her house. At this point, however, we are very happy to impose these negative externalities on others.

> *Q: The city government doesn't care about my skunk problem, and I don't want to pay extra to have the skunk taken out to the suburbs. Is there any way that my neighbors can get together efficiently so that I don't impose this **externality** on them?*

19.10

Travis County is instituting an online jury registration process. Currently, when you are selected for jury duty, you have to go to the local convention center and spend an hour getting in the right line and specifying the times you can serve (or the reasons why you cannot). Every other Monday about 1,000 people trek over to the convention center. With the new process they can specify their availability and get assigned online. The annual cost to the county of setting up and maintaining this service is $300,000. Roughly 25,000 people will avoid spending the time doing this in person. It took me two hours the time I was called, so roughly 50,000 person-hours are spent each year. Let's say that it will take only a half hour to do this online; thus, about 38,000 person-hours will be saved. As long as people's time is valued at more than $8 per hour, this investment is justified. But the county must make the investment. No juryperson could afford to set up the online system on his or her own. This is about as close as we ever come to a new pure **public good.**

> *Q: If this public good were put to a vote—if there were a referendum on spending public funds on it—would you vote yes or no, and why?*

19.11

December 31, 2001—It has been really cold in central Texas, which causes a problem for my wife and me each morning. We use sinks that face each other with a common wall between them. The same hot water pipe supplies the faucets in both sinks. Whoever washes first each morning must put up with two minutes of cold water before the hot water kicks in. This gives me an incentive to wash up second; that way she bears the cost of the cold water and confers a **positive externality** on me. If it were anyone else other than my wife, I'd probably be very careful to go second and be the beneficiary of the **externality.** But because I love my wife and behave **altruistically** toward her, I try to go first as often as I can. Love conquers even economics.

> *Q: What similar externalities exist in your household? Are you as charitable toward the people there as I claim to be toward my wife?*

19.12

A study by a University of Chicago economist caused a furor recently. The economist claimed, with very strong supporting evidence, that the large decline in violent crime in the United States between the mid-1980s and the late 1990s was due in part to the rise in abortions that occurred over the 1970s. The argument is that the aborted fetuses would in many cases have grown up to commit crimes. We also know that crime is highly seasonal, with violent crime rates rising in periods of hot weather. Perhaps having air-conditioning in many more residences beginning in the 1980s reduced potential criminals' incentives to go out onto hot streets to mug, rob, rape, or murder. After all, we believe that one of the main reasons industry moved south and west starting in the 1960s was the ability to make those areas more habitable in the summer. Might the growth of air-conditioning have produced a **positive externality** on crime rates?

> *Q: If this argument for the benefits of air-conditioning is correct and air-conditioning generates positive externalities in the form of reductions in crime rates, should the federal government intervene in the market to subsidize the purchase of air conditioners?*

19.13

February 3, 2002—As of Friday airline tickets have increased up to $5 each way to pay for heightened airport security. The airline industry and a passengers' advocacy group argued that the government should pay this fee, not those who travel. What **externality** would justify making the average taxpayer pay for this service? What **transaction costs** make it difficult to collect the fee? There are none: The only beneficiaries are those people who fly, and since airline taxes are already figured into the price of a ticket, it is costless to add another $5 in fees. This was a blatant attempt by the beneficiaries of a government service to get others to pay for it.

> *Q: Can you think of any arguments showing how the general taxpayer who flies rarely might benefit from increased airline security and thus reasonably be expected to pay part of the costs of airport security?*

19.14

The University of Texas requires me to obtain approval from the Board of Regents of the University to use this book in my micro principles class. I will do so, but I still feel bad about compelling my students to buy it when I stand to make money from their purchases. The ideal thing to do would be to have the publisher charge my own students less. Alternatively, I could personally give all of my 500 students a refund if they show me that they purchased a new copy of the book. The problem is that both of these attempts to assuage my feelings of guilt generate huge **transaction costs** that make them impractical. The only reasonable solution is for me to donate the money from my students' purchases to some cause that the students would approve of, probably an endowment that benefits the university generally.

> *Q: Why not solve the "problem" by holding a large party for all the students right after the final exam?*

19.15

February 5, 2002—A number of people are complaining about the low level of the monetary compensation that they will receive from the federal government for their relatives who were killed in the September 11 terrorist attacks. One gentleman made an extremely clever, although possibly self-serving, comment, stating, "If the government sets a value of life this low, it will affect future calculations about safety improvements." He pointed out that if the government can set a low value of life in safety calculations, the benefits of improving safety—reducing the risk of death in, for example, airplane crashes—will not be seen as sufficient to justify the cost of improving safety. The choices made today, even though they seem specific to the issue of victim compensation, create **externalities** for future discussions of seemingly unrelated issues involving choices made by government agencies.

> *Q: The gentleman is claiming that today's decision imposes an externality through its effects on social choices in the future. How can the government avoid the problem and not let today's decision about compensation create an externality that affects future decisions?*

19.16

Public Goods within the Family. I was talking with my sister about my visit to my parents to spend their wedding anniversary with them last weekend. She said that the visit got points for all three of us (my brother, her, and me) and that she was very grateful that I went. I am glad that my efforts help all three of us (and even more glad that my parents were pleased). I wonder, however, what kind of incentive my visit creates for my siblings: If all three of us get equal praise from the parents if any one of us visits, there is a tremendous incentive for each of us to **free-ride** on the others. I hope, therefore, that my sister was also correct in saying that I got more points from my parents as a result of the trip than did my brother or she. That way visits to parents are at least partly a private good too.

> *Q: What would be the outcome if my parents felt equally "warm and fuzzy" about all three of their children whenever any one of them visited? If my parents are good game theorists and want to have their children visit as often as possible, what should they do to keep this from happening?*

19.17

February 14, 2002—I received a forwarded e-mail listing twenty-two supposedly clever pickup lines by economists for Valentine's Day. Some can't be repeated in polite society, but one polite one is, "Your presence is a big **positive externality.**" Now that is certainly possible, but one would hope that one's spouse or lover's presence is a big positive externality only for oneself. If he or she were a big positive externality for many other people, there would be a tremendous amount of fighting over the spouse or lover's affections.

> *Q: List three real-world goods or activities that may represent a much bigger positive externality, or **negative externality** for one person than for anybody else.*

19.18

There was a disgusting sight on the freeway this morning: a very bloodied, mangled body of an animal. Whoever hit it, and it must have been several people, imposed severe **negative externalities** on people like me who drove by later. The **externalities** could have been ended if the city had simply sent out a crew to clean up the mess. But if the crew had cleaned it up, it would have had to stop traffic, causing traffic jams and imposing a different negative externality on drivers, namely, the time wasted while waiting for the traffic jams to clear up. Which negative externality is more severe, the sight of the dead animal or the time lost waiting for the cleanup? Most people would be more bothered by the time lost, which is why the city typically cleans up street messes at night. Regardless of when the city cleans up a mess, though, one negative externality must be imposed in order to remove another. The person who hit the poor animal forced society into a **trade-off** between two negative externalities.

> *Q: How would you measure the cost of these negative externalities to society: the disgust at seeing the dead animal and the drivers' time lost waiting in traffic while the mess is cleaned up? How would you personally value the two negative externalities?*

19.19

It's a Bad Externality That Does No Good. Two guys riding Harleys zoomed onto the freeway entrance in front of me at sixty miles per hour. They seemed to be likely candidates for death at an early age. I was depressed thinking about the prospect of their demise. No doubt they have families, and as the poet said, every man's death diminishes me. Also, their crazy driving increases the risk of my having an accident as I slam on the brakes to avoid them. There is a bright side that diminishes the **negative externality** that they are imposing on me and on the rest of society: They were not wearing helmets (which are suggested but not required in Texas). This means that should they succeed in crashing, there is a strong possibility that they will be able to function as organ donors, helping to preserve the life of a desperately ill citizen with better sense than they have. Perhaps they recognize this silver lining in the cloud of their negative externality. Perhaps they rationalize their choice of not wearing a helmet both by the freedom they feel and the knowledge that they will do some good after death.

> *Q: These motorcycle drivers create a **positive externality** in the form of the organs they eventually will donate. Do they create any negative externalities?*

19.20

We were attending a wedding on an island just off the South Texas shore. The whole island is a development of expensive houses, most with boat docks. It was windy, and the wind was whipping the spray across the main road. I asked another wedding guest, one who lives in a nearby city, "What happens in a hurricane?" He laughed and said, "The houses are underwater, and there's lots of damage. But don't worry, the federal government helps the people get flood insurance." Federal **subsidies** may make sense to bail out people from unforeseen bad occurrences, but anyone locating on this island (and other islands and seaside locations) knows full well that he or she is prone to hurricane and storm flooding. Why should the average taxpayer subsidize flood insurance for this well-known risk? Worse still, the existence of subsidized flood insurance is a subsidy to construction along these coasts and thus encourages people to put up more buildings there than they would otherwise. It helps demolish wetlands and degrade the environment. Here is a case where the federal government creates a **negative externality** as well as subsidizing people who are typically in the upper part of the income distribution, since those are generally the people who can afford beachfront and nearby property.

> *Q: Without abolishing this subsidized insurance, what would be the effect of a proposal to raise insurance rates in areas where substantial flood damage has occurred recently?*

19.21

As I do before each midterm and final exam in an undergraduate class, I held what was supposed to be a one-and-a-half-hour question and answer (Q&A) session for my students this evening. This is not a review session: Unless the students have questions, I don't say anything. The problem is that most of the students came there without questions, hoping that their fellow students will have questions prepared and that my answers will enlighten everyone. Each student relies on the others, hoping to reap the benefits of the **public good** that is created by my answers. But each student, not wishing to spend time making up questions, becomes a **free rider** on the other students. Today this resulted in very few students bringing in questions. After fifty minutes and a lot of long pauses, I ended the Q&A session. I hope that the students remember what happened in this session when the Q&A for the final exam takes place. The public good problem in this case lasts over two periods of time. If the students realize the longer-term nature of the public good problem here, maybe they will be less interested in free riding off their fellow students next time.

> *Q: What, if any, are the incentives for the students to bring in more questions in the Q&A session before the final exam? Are they greater or less than the incentives were in the midterm Q&A session?*

19.22

During my two months of teaching in Moscow in 1993 I lived in a two-bedroom apartment owned by a former professor of the history of communism. The apartment, one of many in a sixteen-story apartment block, was immaculately clean inside. So too were the apartments of the neighbors who offered me tremendous hospitality (and copious amounts of vodka). The stairwell, however, was filthy, and the small lobby was filled with garbage, old newspapers, and dog poop. Why the difference? Simple: Each household was responsible for its own apartment, but nobody "owned" the lobby; the lobby was a common property resource not owned by anyone. No single household gained enough from keeping it clean to spend time and money cleaning it. The building hadn't yet been privatized, and the Russian government also had no interest in maintaining it. The only encouraging sign was that near the end of my stay, the apartment "owners" had scheduled a meeting to devise some plan to clean up the common areas.

> *Q: Let's say the neighbors agreed to a schedule for keeping the lobby clean. Even with the agreement, how can they solve the **public good** problem discussed here if nobody "owns" the lobby?*

19.23

We bought the coolest techno-toy last weekend: a large digital clock that automatically sets itself every day to the official government atomic clocks. Not being on time generates more **negative externalities** than perhaps anything else we do: If we are not on time, someone else has wasted his or her time waiting for us. If a worker in a group is not on time, the entire group's productivity is diminished. A major distinguishing feature of advanced economies is that people expect each other to be nearly on time for work, meetings, and the like. Without that, the coordination of activities that characterizes those economies would not occur. The clock we purchased is just part of ours, and society's, increasing efforts to keep "on time" and to reduce still further the negative externalities that can arise from failure to coordinate.

> *Q: Are there any negative effects of having everyone be on time? Does the coordination itself induce a negative externality in the form of people behaving as if they were in a rat race?*

19.24

March 27, 2002—A story on the Web today announced that the town of Ridgefield, New Jersey, took a townwide "time-out" yesterday. All after-school, sports, and other activities were canceled, allowing families in this ritzy suburb a time for togetherness. Why is this necessary? Why can't each family take its own time-out? If one family doesn't participate, it loses out on the activity and in some ways falls behind others: The kids don't make the soccer team, Dad doesn't get the lead role in the Easter pageant, and Mom doesn't develop her softball skills. This is what economists call a **coordination problem.** The only way to get people to relax and get a bit less stressful leisure is to have some agreement imposed that ensures that people who don't participate in organized activities on that day do not lose out. The coordination required can't be created by one individual's decision, only by everyone agreeing, because some central authority requires it, to take it easy for some length of time.

> *Q: Is this the same as when a parent requires his or her child to take a "time-out" because the child has misbehaved? Why or why not?*

19.25

An economist from Rio de Janeiro tells me how pretty his home is. He's ten minutes from the beach, but the ocean is completely polluted and he can't swim there. The reason is that the nearby municipality disposes its raw sewage by building very long pipes that take the sewage way out into the ocean. While the sewage is thus removed from that municipality, ocean currents eventually bring it back onto the beaches of nearby areas, including this economist's area. It doesn't pay the municipality to build a treatment plant for the sewage. Removing it by building a long pipeline is cheaper, and imposing **negative externalities** is cheaper. The benefits to the entire metropolitan area if they treated sewage—if they internalized the externalities—almost certainly exceed the costs of building a treatment plant. But no one area benefits enough from the treatment to justify building a treatment plant that would make the entire metropolitan region better off.

Q: What can the Brazilian national government do to solve the problem outlined in this vignette?

19.26

Economists at Play. Nine of us have taken a jungle canopy tour this morning, and twelve other people are along. The tour is taking a long time, and we have to be at the dock to go on a sailing trip at 1:30 PM. Worse, the tour company promises a swim in a jungle pool after the canopy tour, something none of us economists wants to do. One economist suggests that we bribe the other people to give up their swim so that we can get back to town earlier. Another notes that because they have **property rights** to the swim—it was advertised as part of the tour—and know that we're in a hurry, they will overstate the amount they would require to give up their swim. Yet another economist points out that it's a shame that the swim was included in the tour, since the others could not have paid us enough for the swim to compensate for our impatience to get back to town. An initial grant of property rights has a tremendous impact on distribution. If there are **transaction costs,** as there are in this case, issues of bargaining and bluffing may prevent people from achieving a **Pareto optimum.**

Q: There were two buses taking the group. Is there any way that both the economists and the others could be made better off?

19.27

Out-of-state students at the University of Texas pay much higher tuition than do in-state students. But the extra tuition **revenues** are kept by the state of Texas, not by the university. University officials today said that they would like to have more out-of-state students (only 9 percent of undergraduates are not Texans), but why bother? The university doesn't retain the tuition revenues, and out-of-staters take places away from Texans. Despite these disincentives, officials argue that the presence of out-of-state students enriches the university experience for Texans, that the presence of out-of-staters on campus creates **positive externalities** for Texas students. Perhaps so, but is the value of this positive externality high enough to justify using scarce places on campus for these students? If the university were allowed to keep the extra tuition revenue these students generate—if it could internalize the monetary as well as the nonmonetary benefits—this positive externality might be worth capturing.

> *Q: If you were a state legislator from North Zulch, Texas, how would you react to the university's concerns? What if you were an alumnus of the university who no longer resided in Texas?*

19.28

Over the years some citizens have lobbied for the enactment of "takings" laws. These laws would require governments to compensate fully anyone whose property interests are harmed by government actions that generate **negative externalities**. Presumably these efforts stem from a belief that compensation under rules of eminent domain—when government takes private property for public use—has been insufficient. Perhaps so, but to be fair the same people should also be pushing "givings" laws that would require those who benefit from the **positive externalities** arising from government decisions about land use to pay all their excess gains back in higher property taxes. Each landowner whose previously worthless property suddenly becomes a prime location for a motel or gas station when a highway interchange or airport is built should pay a tax equal to the amount by which the land has risen in value. If it makes sense to compensate for negative externalities, it makes sense to compensate for positive externalities too.

> *Q: Is there any reason why it might be harder to measure the gains from the positive externalities than to measure the losses from the negative externalities?*

19.29

Does an increased population degrade the lifestyle of the world's citizens? Not necessarily. A larger population does put more demands on the environment, including more potential problems such as global warming and the destruction of rain forests. But a larger population also means more total benefits from the creation of knowledge and thus more incentive to generate that knowledge and bring its fruits to market. A drug company or a government may not want to incur the **fixed cost** of developing a cure for a rare disease that affects 0.1 percent of a population of one billion people. They are more likely to do so if the disease afflicts 0.1 percent of a population of ten billion. Obversely, with a larger population any negative impact of an economic activity affects more people and generates a greater willingness to pay to reduce or eliminate that detrimental activity.

> *Q: What does a reduction in international transportation costs do to a company's willingness to undertake research that might generate a drug that might cure a rare disease?*

19.30

Grackles infesting Austin have become a year-round problem. They generate only **negative externalities:** They are noisy, they swoop by as one is walking, and their droppings in parking lots have created a tremendous demand for car washes in the city, thus helping waste scarce water supplies. They have no redeeming value. One might think the same would be true of the local bat colony. A half million of these flying mammals migrate from Mexico to Austin each spring, take up residence under a downtown bridge, and give birth to their pups. Unlike the grackles, their annual evening outings to hunt for food are a minor tourist attraction, and by preying on insects they help keep other pests under control. They generate substantial **positive externalities**.

> *Q: Think about nonnative animals and insects where you live. Which ones generate positive, and which ones negative, externalities?*

CHAPTER 20

Taxes and Public Expenditures

20.1

In the Beatles song the "Tax Man" sings, "There's one for you, nineteen for me." The Beatles are complaining about the high **marginal tax rate** that they faced in the United Kingdom in the 1960s. Implicitly each extra pound that they earned left them only five pence (one-twentieth of a pound), with the remaining ninety-five pence going to the tax collector. This is clearly about the marginal tax rate, the tax on each extra bit of earnings, not the average tax rate, the ratio of taxes to total income. No tax system has an average tax rate of 95 percent on the entire tax base. The 95 percent marginal rate is also probably an exaggeration: Most systems have loopholes that allow some income to escape taxation when the rate is this steep. That Sir Paul McCartney is now a billionaire is pretty good evidence that the Beatles never really paid 95 percent of their earnings in taxes.

> *Q: What is the marginal tax rate on your earnings if you are working? What is your parent(s)' marginal tax rate? Are these the same as the average tax rates?*

20.2

November 26, 2001—It's not often that the incidence of a tax is obviously split between producers and consumers, as the textbooks would suggest is the case. But on the day when the U.S. government reimposed a 10 percent tax on airline tickets, some of the airlines tried to increase fares by 10 percent. Others did not go along, however, and later in the day the companies dropped their fares to 4 percent above where they had been the day before (before the tax was reimposed). The fare increase settled at 4 percent. The consumer paid 40 percent of the new tax, and the producers paid 60 percent—even though the tax was imposed initially on the companies.

> *Q: Draw a supply-demand graph in the market for airline tickets. Draw the **demand curve** in such a way that it generates a 4 percent increase in the **equilibrium price** after a 10 percent shift in supply. How must you draw the demand and supply curves to get this result?*

20.3

The states got a settlement from tobacco companies totaling several hundred billion dollars over a 25-year period. The settlement money is supposed to be used for smoking prevention and/or education. Perhaps unsurprisingly, only 5 percent has been used for those purposes. The states seem to be using most of the money to reduce taxes. In one of the most goofy incentives ever set up, the amount that some of the states will get is higher if smoking rates fail to drop.

> *Q: What incentives can the courts give the states to use the settlement money in a way that helps reduce smoking?*

20.4

In introductory micro classes we make the assumption that consumers maximize utility and firms maximize profits. What do governments maximize? This question has bothered economists and others for a long time, and attempts to answer it have led to one Nobel Prize in economics. One simple thought is that in their operations governments minimize costs. Another is that each regime in a democratic society reflects the will of the marginal (or median) voter, the person whose choice in the next election determines whether the incumbents or their opponents win. To me both of these explanations seem even more oversimplified than our assumptions about maximization by firms or consumers; even a local government seems too diverse to have its behavior characterized this way. But we need some assumption to capture government behavior; just talking about it is not very useful.

> *Q: Others suggest that governments maximize the interests of the elected officials, subject to the constraint that the officials wish to be reelected. How might a government maximizing this way provide garbage collection services differently from one that tries to minimize costs? How about national defense?*

20.5

Newspapers are full of stories about companies that offer to locate in a state or city in exchange for tax breaks: no state corporate income taxes or local property taxes for an extended period of time. Others add direct **subsidies** in their requests to state and local governments. Perhaps the most visible claimants are professional sports franchises. Do these subsidies pay off for taxpayers? A reasonable criterion is that the discounted value of the extra taxes generated by the extra business and jobs created should at least equal the tax breaks and subsidies offered to the companies. I doubt that governments do much better than this breakeven level. The reason is that the companies and sports franchises behave like **monopolists** in bargaining with the various governments that are competing to get a company to locate. As monopolists bargaining with competing governments, they can extract, in the form of tax breaks, every bit of **economic rent** that the locality might have gotten from the deal. Sports franchises do even better: Citizens seem willing to pay higher taxes or give up public services for the prestige of having a major-league sports franchise in the city.

> *Q: How would the amount of tax breaks that are offered change if the company was one that needed to use particular mineral resources that are located in only two places in the United States? Why does this outcome differ from the one described in the vignette?*

20.6

December 6, 2001—A story in yesterday's *Wall Street Journal* talked about President Bush's proposal to allow people who take the standard deduction on their income taxes to itemize their charitable contributions and deduct them from their Adjusted Gross Income (AGI). This would give low-income taxpayers, the people who generally use the standard deduction, a bigger tax break if they contributed to charities. Law professors don't like this, arguing that the standard deduction already accounts for charitable contributions. Economists say it wouldn't have much effect. The reason is that the price of a $1 charitable contribution is $[1 − t]$, where t is a household's **marginal tax rate.** Low-income households taking the standard deduction face a tax rate of only 0.15. The deduction wouldn't reduce the price of giving to charity very much for them.

> *Q: Say the **price elasticity of demand** for giving to charity is −2. What is the impact on their charitable contributions if we make charitable contributions tax-deductible for low-income households facing a tax rate of 0.15?*

20.7

While I was walking through the airport today with my parents and older son, as we passed Southwest Airlines, my mother remarked that she thought they were bankrupt. I said that to the contrary, they are the only airline that made a profit during the most recent quarter. My son said that I was wrong and that Midway Airlines made a profit. I asked how that could be. He said that they were indeed bankrupt, were not operating at all during that time, and thus had no operating expenses. However, as part of the airline bailout they received federal funds this fall. It is impossible to defend this giveaway on any **efficiency** grounds. On **equity** grounds, unless one believes that the share-holders of this company are worthy recipients of a redistribution of funds from the general public, there is no defense either.

> *Q: What evidence would you need to support an argument that providing a bailout to Midway Airlines might be justifiable on equity grounds?*

20.8

January 12, 2002—This week the Immigration and Naturalization Service (INS) of the federal government is beginning efforts to deport some of the nearly 300,000 people whose visas have expired and who are subject to deportation. The INS is beginning by focusing on Middle Eastern men. Whether this is fair is unclear. It may be sensible economically, though, if illegal aliens of different ethnic groups concentrate in particular localities so that there are **economies of scale** that arise from concentrating on one or two groups. As a taxpayer I find this argument for **efficiency** in government appealing. As a citizen concerned about **equity,** I find it not quite so appealing.

> *Q: The issue in this vignette is one of targeting government resources. Violations of laws regulating overtime hours (time-and-a-half pay for hours beyond forty per week) represent another area where the government can inspect or investigate only a small fraction of the potential violators. How should the government economize on its resources in this area? How is the problem in that case different from the problem in targeting illegal aliens?*

20.9

In a pay-as-you-go social security system such as the one in the United States old-age benefits are financed by payroll taxes on today's workers and employers. An economist presented her study examining a reform in the Mexican social security system. Mexico has partially privatized its system, investing some of the employer's payroll taxes in the equivalent of Individual Retirement Accounts—savings that are invested to build up a retirement income for you. Each younger worker will have part of his or her pension coming from these IRA-like sources rather than out of a pay-as-you-go system. How valuable is this switch? That is, does the individual worker value the marginal dollar (peso, actually) of taxes put aside in his or her IRA more or less than a similar peso put into a pay-as-you-go plan? The estimates suggest that Mexican workers view the peso put into the IRA equivalent as more desirable than the peso put into a pay-as-you-go system. Workers would be willing to pay extra for a plan in which their taxes are linked to them specifically than for a pay-as-you-go plan like social security. Whether the same results would be found for the United States is not clear, but they do suggest some good arguments for at least partial privatization of the U.S. social security system.

Q: Say you are offered today $1 in extra social security benefits when you reach sixty-five or $1 from an IRA that you have controlled all your life. Which would you prefer? How would your answer change if it were $0.50 from the IRA?

20.10

February 7, 2002—Last year the United States enacted a massive tax cut programmed to become effective over the next eight years. The tax cut includes the abolition of the federal tax on estates left when someone dies. The cut is not permanent: Taxes will revert to their 2000 levels after 2010. President Bush, as part of his new economic stimulus package, included a provision to make it permanent. That was just killed in the Senate. Now, why should anyone fight over this? Even if the tax cut were permanent, the permanent status could be repealed in 2010; similarly, the cuts could be made permanent in 2010 if Congress then wished to. Politicians must believe that decisions about taxes are asymmetric: It's much harder to defend a vote to abolish a permanent tax cut that has been enacted than it is to ignore it when previous tax cuts lapse. This speaks more to the shortsightedness of voters than to any kind of setting of taxes in accordance with national priorities.

Q: If you were a multimillionaire thinking about estate taxes, would you hold on to your estate until 2011 and take a chance that the repeal of the estate tax will become permanent? Or would you get rid of much of it before then to take advantage of what may be temporarily low estate taxes? What considerations other than taxes affect your decision?

20.11

Higher education spending by state and local governments was $9.97 per $1,000 of personal income in their states in fiscal year 1982, $8.24 per $1,000 in fiscal year 1992, and only $7.67 per $1,000 in fiscal year 2002. As income has gone up, government spending has failed to increase as rapidly, a result presumably determined by decisions of voters about how much governments should spend on this service. Although probably not an **inferior good,** public support of higher education is clearly a **necessity,** not a **luxury.** At the same time, we know that higher-income people spend proportionately more of their income on higher education; it is a luxury good at the personal level. Why the difference between the personal and the public? The marginal voter who determines how much is spent on this activity by the government must have a lower **income elasticity of demand** than the average person who chooses how much to spend out of his or her own income.

> *Q: Look around you in class and ask whether the typical student in your school comes from a family with income above or below the average in your state. (National average family income today is not much more than $50,000.) What does your answer tell you about the income elasticity of demand for higher education at your institution?*

20.12

The city government offers rebates to residents who purchase and install a new, more energy-efficient clothes-washing machine. The private company that supplies natural gas will add to the rebate if the washing machine uses water heated by a gas-fired hot-water heater. The purpose of the **subsidies** is to encourage reduced energy usage. This offer is amazing: How many private companies would give you a subsidy to use less of their product? Although energy conservation is a fine goal, is this kind of subsidy, which requires customers to fill out paperwork and have a city inspection, the most efficient way to conserve natural resources? Why don't they just charge higher prices for natural gas? Why don't the city and state impose a tax on natural gas usage if they are serious about conservation? These alternatives would reduce energy use without wasting nonenergy resources: bureaucrats' and citizens' time.

> *Q: Assume that the **price elasticity of demand** for washing machines is −0.5. If the city offers a 10 percent **subsidy,** by how much will the number of washing machines sold increase?*

20.13

The state of Washington had imposed a licensing fee on cars that rose as a car's value increased. Fees on cars valued at more than $25,000 amounted to $600 per year. A referendum reduced this to a flat fee of $30 per car. Now, why would the average voter approve replacing a clearly **progressive tax** with a fixed-amount, obviously **regressive tax?** Either the average voter is dumb, not realizing that this hurts him or her and helps the rich, or he or she believes that by cutting one tax there will be no offsetting increases in other taxes. Appealing to the average person to help reduce a tax that hits mainly the rich is a common ploy. A good example is the pressure brought (successfully) on Congress several years ago to repeal a special excise tax on boats costing more than $30,000. The argument was that the tax hurt the workers in the boat-building industry. Possibly so, but it requires a strange theory of **tax incidence** for that to be true.

> *Q: If you had been in the state of Washington at that time, would you have voted to repeal the tax? How would the repeal have helped or hurt you, and how does that affect your opinion on the fee referendum?*

20.14

A legislator in California has proposed putting heavy taxes on soft drinks and candy bars. Her ostensible purpose is to discourage people from consuming products that contribute to obesity. She views obesity as a burden on the public, since it leads to more circulatory disease. The public interest, she would argue, requires this, since such disease imposes a **negative externality** on taxpayers who fund the state Medicaid systems that take care of many poor people's health problems. This is exactly the same argument that was used to justify the tobacco settlement, in which tobacco companies agreed in the late 1990s to compensate state governments. Here "compensation" will be paid by candy bar and soft drink addicts who continue to buy the products even after the prices rise in response to the imposition of the tax. Unfortunately, as is true with so many "sin" taxes, the **income elasticity of demand** for these goods is low: They are necessities. That means that the burden of the tax will fall heavily on lower-income consumers: The tax will be a **regressive tax.**

> *Q: How about instead arguing that dinners at any restaurant whose meals cost more than $30 per head are likely to be fatty and deserve to be curtailed. Would the effect on health be the same? Would the burden by income class be the same?*

20.15

February 20, 2002—A headline in the Raleigh, North Carolina, *News and Observer* dealing with possible tax increases to finance higher education reads, "Mill workers making $25K must sacrifice to help faculty making $100K." The average faculty member in North Carolina makes less than $100K. The average taxpayer makes more than $25K but probably does earn less than the average faculty member. The issue is not really taxpayers versus faculty members. It's taxpayers (who finance public higher education) versus the families of students enrolled in higher education. To the extent that students come from richer families than those of the average taxpayer, using tax dollars to finance public higher education represents a **regressive** transfer. If the **income elasticity of demand** for higher education is higher than the income elasticity of the state's tax base, raising tuition makes the burden of supporting higher education more **progressive.**

> *Q: Assume that the income elasticity of demand for higher education is +2, a family with an income of $50,000 spends $3,000 on higher education, and state taxes are always 10 percent of income. How does the burden of higher education on a family making $50,000 compare with that on a family making $100,000?*

20.16

New property tax assessments are arriving soon. For many residents the increase in the tax will represent a 20 percent rise over two years ago. Many property owners find this really annoying; and, if they don't think about it, they would love to see some other tax replace the property tax. In response to such complaints many states have substituted other taxes, especially sales tax increases, and reduced property taxes. Property taxes are a tax on the demand for housing. The **income elasticity of demand** is higher than it is for most goods subject to sales taxes unless the sales tax exempts enough **necessities.** A general sales tax is thus **regressive** compared to a property tax. Substituting a general sales tax for property taxes reduces **equity** in taxation.

> *Q: In the game Monopoly there is a $75 luxury tax, with a picture of a diamond ring. Why don't modern governments solve this problem of taxation by replacing property, income, and sales taxes*

with taxes on only diamond rings, yachts, Mercedes-Benz and Jaguar cars, and the like?

20.17

The Internal Revenue Service has ruled that spending for weight-loss activities is deductible from personal income taxes as a medical expense. By declaring this spending deductible, the IRS is allowing somebody with a 35 percent tax rate to have thirty-five cents of each dollar of spending at, for example, Weight Watchers subsidized by the federal government. Someone with a 15 percent tax rate has fifteen cents of each dollar subsidized. Because the U.S. income tax is a **progressive tax,** the **subsidy** is a bigger percentage gift to the rich than to the poor: The government is doing more to help the rich keep thin than to help the poor! The subsidy has other effects. It increases the demand for weight-loss services, helping companies like Weight Watchers. And people who are employed by Weight Watchers, such as Sarah Ferguson, Duchess of York, who advertises for them, are likely to see an increased demand for their services.

> *Q: The IRS does not allow people to deduct memberships in health clubs from their adjusted gross incomes in figuring their tax liability. How does this difference affect the demand for weight-loss programs relative to the demand for health clubs?*

20.18

Costa Rica, like many smaller countries, charges a departure tax at its international airport. I pay a $17 tax, but Costa Rican citizens pay $41 and resident noncitizens pay $61. Why charge foreigners less? The issue is tax competition. As a small country competing for business and tourists, Costa Rica can't charge a huge amount. If it did, travelers, knowing this, would go elsewhere. Its own citizens have little choice: This is the only way they can exit the country conveniently. Moreover, given the amount of tax evasion, a departure tax is a good way to collect taxes, and it is fairly **progressive:** Richer Costa Ricans fly out of the country more often than do their poorer fellow citizens. The $61 tax on residents must be demand-based **price discrimination** against people who have an even lower **price elasticity of demand** for departures than citizens do—probably wealthy foreigners who make their homes in Costa Rica but maintain other citizenship.

> *Q: Why not charge resident foreigners a $1,000 tax each time they depart the country?*

20.19

Several years ago the state of Texas surprised the public by creating a tax holiday the weekend before school started. School supplies, kids' clothing, and related items were temporarily exempted from the 8 percent state sales tax. Who really benefited from the tax holiday? What was the **tax incidence** of this temporary tax cut? That depended on how the supply and demand for these items responded to the tax cut and the resulting drop in the net price. It's hard to believe that demand responded much because by that weekend many people had already bought the back-to-school items. If not, they had to buy them then—an **inelastic demand**. That would have led to a big drop in the net price: Consumers reaped most of the benefit from the tax holiday. Since then the state has been offering this holiday annually, and most people expect it. They are adjusting their spending patterns accordingly so that now there is a more **elastic demand** on that weekend. Retail stores too can plan around this date all year long and be sure that they reap part of the gains from the temporary—but now fully anticipated—tax holiday. Buyers and sellers now share the incidence of the tax cut.

> *Q: If you want to make sure that consumers get the benefits of the tax cut—that the incidence is entirely on them—how can you design tax holidays to do this?*

CHAPTER 21

International Economics

21.1

While I was checking in at American Airlines in Austin yesterday, the CEO of that company was in the airport shaking hands with employees. Amazing—the CEO of a major company spurring on the workers! The woman checking me in was less impressed. She remarked that she bet that he couldn't check me in. I didn't raise the question with her, but I wondered whether customers would want him to be able to do this. Aren't the company and its stockholders better off if each employee's **comparative advantage** is used—if it takes advantage of the gains to specialization? The CEO's time is better spent thinking about how to run the company more effectively, not learning how to do every job in the company.

> *Q: In some industries and activities specialization makes more sense than it does in others. Describe the kinds of companies in which the comparative advantage of workers is more or less important.*

21.2

Electricité de France, the heavily subsidized government-owned French power company, is trying to move into foreign markets, including that of Great Britain. The British government is complaining that this will represent unfair competition for its companies. Should average Britons be upset? Quite the contrary— they should welcome this. The competition will lower the prices they pay for electricity in two ways. The additional competition will force domestic firms to cut prices to compete. Also, to continue making profits in the face of lower prices, domestic firms will be forced to become more efficient through both better management and more innovation. The British consumer should be thanking the French public for its willingness to waste its funds by **subsidizing** a company that is willing to sell its power so cheaply so that British citizens may benefit.

> *Q: If you were an average French citizen, how would you feel about Electricité de France selling subsidized power in Britain? How would you feel if you were a worker in this company?*

21.3

It is laundry time in our house. The problem is that I am hopeless at deciding what clothes to wash together and what must be dried outside the clothes dryer. But I work at home a lot, unlike my wife, and thus have time to move the loads from the washer to the dryer and then into the laundry basket. I'm also capable of the unskilled labor of folding my own clothes. Therefore, my wife separates the laundry into piles (the skilled work), instructs me to put them into the washer in sequence, and indicates which items should not go into the dryer. This system, which took years to develop, has ended my practice of creating colored, formerly white underwear. This routine is our biweekly exercise in using the principle of **comparative advantage** in the household.

> *Q: List an activity in which you and your roommate(s) use the principle of comparative advantage to split the duties to maximize the well-being of your household. How have your comparative advantages in different activities changed over the time you have been together?*

21.4

The laundry tasks are reminiscent of a couple we knew many years ago, Louie and Sheri. Sheri was very proud that each of them did his or her own laundry entirely separately. I thought this was very silly, as it failed to spread the **fixed cost** of starting up the wash, moving it to the dryer, and carrying it back. It seemed to be a waste of time, although Sheri was insistent that they both wanted their independence. Marriage benefits from the **comparative advantage** of the spouses in different activities, and it also benefits from **economies of scale** in producing many of the activities done at home.

> *Q: Discuss the specifics of comparative advantage in the household in the case of meal preparation and cleanup.*

21.5

The man in the next seat on a recent airplane trip starting chatting with me, found out I am an economist, and asked the following question, "I am a regional vice president for a large food-service company. We were just taken over by a huge British company that owns a variety of food-industry businesses. What is the net benefit of this internationalization for the U.S. economy?" It probably does not make very much difference for the U.S. economy. On the benefit side, the British firm bought his company because it believed it could run the company more efficiently. Presumably this will generate lower costs and, in this fairly competitive industry, lower prices to the American consumer. A negative effect might be that the profits from the American business, which previously might have generated purchasing power in the United States, will now go to British owners and raise purchasing power there. Perhaps a more important negative is that regional VPs might now see their career paths blocked unless they are willing to become more internationally oriented.

> *Q: List businesses for which this kind of merger would have larger effects on the U.S. economy. List some where the effects are likely to be even smaller.*

21.6

We bought a jar of dill pickles today with the brand name Zergüt. Since the label depicts the often-photographed Bavarian castle at Neuschwanstein, this name is presumably a (purposeful?) corruption of the German *Sehr gut* ("very good"), although the reason for the misspelling is unclear. The label also calls the product "Russian-style dill pickles," and the product is made in Bulgaria.

With declining transportation costs and other decreases in the costs of marketing, we will no doubt see still more such mixed-up products. We are no doubt better off because unlike people of previous generations, we can buy Zergüt pickles. It would be nice, though, if the benefits of this increased **globalization** were not partly offset by the absurdities of labels like these.

> *Q: Are there any cases in which you or I should care where a product is made as long as we want it and it offers the best quality for the price?*

21.7

One of my pesky colleagues has mentioned several times that my website has "broken links," whatever that means. Apparently the little pictures that people are supposed to click on are not there. He says it is simply a matter of adding two files. Now, I know nothing about this, but I have asked our department's computer person to come to my office and take care of the problem. I told this to my colleague, who asked, "Why don't you do it yourself?" I told him that it's not my **absolute advantage** or my **comparative advantage.** I don't know how and don't want to spend time learning; that's why we have the computer consultant. The colleague said that I eventually would be doing this myself. He would be correct only if it takes me less time to do it than it would to ask the consultant to do it.

> *Q: What computer applications would you do yourself, and what would you ask for help on? How are these two types of activities different from each other?*

21.8

The World Economic Forum, a meeting of government leaders, business leaders, and others, opens today. As in the past it will be accompanied by protests by "antiglobalization" groups. I'm never sure what that term means. Is it less pollution, less cross-border ownership of assets, less international trade, or what? If it is less trade, particularly fewer imports, which seems to be the goal of the protests' U.S. trade union supporters, I am reminded of an old cartoon. The first picture shows a well-dressed family sitting around a table in a well-stocked kitchen, with the father saying, "We need to buy American." The second picture shows the same scene with Dad, Mom, and the kids naked; the pots, stove, and curtains missing; and almost nothing else left.

> *Q: Look around your dormitory room or apartment. Make a list of the items that would not be there if international trade was impossible. Ask yourself whether there are U.S.-made substitutes and how desirable they are compared to the imported items you own.*

21.9

In 1991 Colombia tried a new way of "protecting" its industries from foreign competition: It tried to auction off **import quotas.** Economists don't like import quotas. Unlike **tariffs,** which at least put customs receipts in the treasury's coffers, quotas restrict trade while earning taxpayers nothing. Auctioning quotas would seem to solve this problem, since the auction generates receipts for the government. Unfortunately, businesses did not want to bid on the import quotas, and they were undersubscribed. If businesses were perfectly certain about their demand for potential imports and if the red tape were minor, auctions would produce the same patterns of trade as tariffs. That companies didn't want to bid suggests that one or both of these preconditions wasn't met. In any case, Colombia soon abandoned the idea and went back to tariffs.

> *Q: What are the characteristics of companies that are likely to bid more for the rights to import some product? Large or small companies? New or old companies?*

21.10

We got to talking at lunch about differences between Europeans and Americans in sporting activities. This is reminiscent of stories, perhaps apocryphal, that circulated widely during the French riots of 1968 that toppled President de Gaulle. American exchange students were in great demand by the rioters. Because Americans grow up playing baseball while Europeans do not, the Americans were much better at throwing rocks at policemen and at breaking windows than their fellow, European rioters were. This is not a **comparative advantage** that should be cultivated, but it does indicate how investment in **human capital** in one area (sports) can create a comparative advantage in a totally different area (rioting). Perhaps the French used some of their skills to provide pastries to motivate the American rock throwers.

> *Q: If you were organizing a march to protest higher tuition, what kinds of students would you put in front of the march to make it most effective?*

21.11

March 4, 2002—President Bush has until Wednesday to issue an order in response to the U.S. International Trade Commission's finding that foreigners have dumped steel in the United States. He has to do something, especially because he would like to get votes from steelworkers in West Virginia, Pennsylvania, and Ohio in his reelection bid in 2004 and for Republicans in 2002. The problem is that steel users—automobile manufacturers and their workers and others—don't want higher steel prices. Also, the European Union and others will take the United States to the World Trade Organization and seek sanctions if we impose much higher **tariffs** on steel. No matter what he does, it looks like a no-win situation for Bush. In that case, why not do the right thing? Admit that the United States is not very competitive in steel, that we did not respond quickly enough to the sharp loss of **economies of scale** in steel production that occurred in the 1980s and 1990s by adopting new efficient methods. We thus lost out to more efficient foreign producers. If he must slap on a tariff, he should make it the smallest one possible so that U.S. consumers of goods that contain steel aren't hurt very much. Otherwise, this becomes a classic case of protecting inefficient firms and workers at the expense of the consumer.

> *Q: If the tariff is a bad idea economically, why is it so attractive politically?*

21.12

March 6, 2002—President Bush went ahead and authorized **tariffs** on a large variety of imported steel products. Imports from

Mexico and Canada were exempted. The reactions are completely predictable. The Europeans, Koreans, Brazilians, and Japanese are ready to complain to the World Trade Organization that the United States has acted unfairly. Those complaints take years to resolve, though, so they are also contemplating retaliatory tariffs on other U.S. products. The Germans even claimed that they let their own steel industry restructure, so why should they bear the cost of America's unwillingness to let its industry modernize? This kind of fighting is how trade wars get started. Without having to seem like a villain, Canada benefits from the Bush decision, because its steel exports to the United States have less competition. The Canadians can then sell more steel to America and sell it at higher prices. Small wonder that a Canadian official expressed approval of the U.S. actions.

> *Q: You are a typical citizen of a country that neither produces steel nor buys any steel from the United States. Does the new American tariff make you better or worse off, or does it have no effect on you?*

21.13

U.S. candy producers are complaining that the high domestic price of sugar is forcing them to move production abroad, where they can buy sugar at the much lower world price. U.S. sugar growers are heavily protected, and the U.S. price is much higher than the world price. But that has been true for at least forty years. Equilibrium doesn't change unless some underlying factor has changed, so high sugar prices can't be the cause. What has changed is that **tariffs** on manufactured goods have been lowered fairly steadily, particularly within North America under the North American Free Trade Agreement (NAFTA). Since much of the imported candy comes from Canadian plants, lower tariffs (in the case of NAFTA, zero tariffs) seem like the cause of the relocation of candy plants. But the candy manufacturers are correct about one thing: Lowering domestic sugar prices to the world price would reduce the cost disadvantages of producing here and at least partly stem losses in domestic output.

> *Q: What would lowering U.S. sugar prices do to the market value of Canadian candy companies that are potential takeover targets by American firms?*

21.14

Deans and the president are the big shots in a university. They are people the typical student never sees, but they run the institution. They usually come from the ranks of professors. Of course preferences matter: Some professors who would be highly competent administrators prefer to keep teaching and doing research rather than becoming full-time managers even though they would get paid more as managers. Many professors, though, enter teaching and research because they don't enjoy dealing with people and don't like being part of a hierarchy. They could not be managers. A few others may be better than their colleagues at research and teaching too; they may have an **absolute advantage** at teaching and research. But they have greater interpersonal skills and may not be interested in continuing teaching and research. These interpersonal skills are rare among professors, and the few who have them become deans and presidents. Their **comparative advantage** leads them to fill these administrative jobs.

> *Q: Assume that one professor is mediocre at everything—teaching, research, and administration—while another is good at all these things. Which one should the university want to have as an administrator, and which one doing teaching and research?*

21.15

April 10, 2002—The news reports that Levi Strauss, the creator of blue jeans, is closing most of its remaining U.S. manufacturing plants, citing high labor costs in the United States for the fairly unskilled work. It will contract with other companies, mostly in developing countries, for manufacturing and will concentrate on design and marketing. Should we be depressed about this? No. It's a natural example of a process by which the United States produces those goods in which it has a **comparative advantage**— high-tech and innovative products—and lets lower-wage countries produce goods that do not require highly skilled labor. Yes. It's depressing that one of our most famous and oldest brands may not be produced here and that some very senior workers will lose their jobs. The hope is that our programs to compensate displaced workers—unemployment insurance and trade adjustment assistance (TAA)—will help these workers get retrained or at least ease their retirement. Indeed, TAA was designed partly to reduce political pressures against freer trade by people who might be harmed by increased foreign competition.

> *Q: How much compensation should the government give to workers who are displaced by foreign competition? If you ran the federal government, how much would you offer?*

21.16

A local "consumer advocate" is quoted in today's student newspaper: "To promote and support **globalization** is to be a selfish person and care nothing about the welfare of the world." No doubt she feels good saying this, but if globalization means rescuing workers, including very small children, from backbreaking low-productivity farm work and putting them into better-paying although still low-paid industrial work, it is she, not globalizers, who cares "nothing about the welfare of the world." She certainly doesn't care about consumers, American or other. If she did, she would recognize that producing goods for world markets in those countries where production is most efficient helps American consumers (and those of other countries too).

> *Q: What is your reaction to a proposal to aid downtrodden foreign laborers by banning imports of goods produced by workers earning less than the U.S. **minimum wage**?*

21.17

One of America's biggest net export industries is higher education. Many foreign students come to the United States for undergraduate and graduate degrees; few Americans go abroad for their degrees. The reason is simple: Our institutions of higher education are recognized as offering the best education in the world, especially in terms of educating teachers and researchers in graduate programs. What is the gain to the United States of doing this? If a foreign undergraduate student pays tuition in excess of the **marginal cost** of his or her education, the U.S. educational system adds to its surplus. Foreign graduate students may not pay tuition, but they often provide low-cost instruction to undergraduates in U.S. universities. Most important, when those students return home, they carry with them knowledge and a set of attitudes that allow the American approach to economics, and to society, to spread across the world. We export both **human capital** and culture when we educate foreign students.

> *Q: If these benefits are real, why don't we pay foreign undergraduates to attend U.S. universities?*

Tips on Hunting for Economics Everywhere in Part III

1. When someone postpones an activity, what does that imply about the rate of return?
2. Ask yourself why people's wages differ and search for the underlying determinants. Look for differences by demographic group, kinds of activities undertaken, and other potential sources.
3. Examine job hunting by people you know and consider why they accept or fail to accept jobs. What does their behavior imply about their attitudes?
4. Watch for responses to changes in marginal tax rates, especially when the tax rate rises or falls sharply. Look at how behavior differs in response to changes in average and marginal rates.
5. Look for cases where the activity of a person, firm, or company affects the well-being of others in surprising ways. Look for both positive and negative externalities.
6. Consider how outcomes differ depending on who has property rights. How do groups try to overcome initial grants of property rights?
7. Look for instances of the use of comparative advantage in your own activities and in changing patterns of international trade.

Glossary

Absolute advantage   Higher actual productivity than other producers.

Addiction   Increasing satisfaction from a good resulting from prior consumption of that good.

Altruism   Deriving satisfaction from increases in the satisfaction of someone else.

Antitrust   Policies or activities designed to limit monopoly or oligopoly power in a market.

Average fixed cost   Total fixed cost divided by the number of units produced.

Average product   The ratio of output to the quantity of an input.

Average tax rate   Total taxes divided by the total amount that is taxed.

Average total cost   Total cost (fixed plus variable) divided by the number of units produced.

Average variable cost   Total variable cost divided by the number of units produced.

Bilateral monopoly   A market relationship in which the seller has monopoly power and the buyer has monopsony power.

Change in demand   A shift in the amount people wish to buy at any given price; usually due to changes in income, prices of related goods, tastes, or market size.

Comparative advantage   Relatively greater productivity in an activity.

Compensating wage differential   Extra pay for an unpleasant aspect of an occupation.

Competitive equilibrium   A situation in a competitive market in which no firms have an incentive to enter or exit because there is no economic profit.

Complements   A pair of goods related so that when the price of one falls, the amount of the other sold rises.

Consumer demand   The quantity customers wish to buy.

Consumer surplus   The excess of the amount consumers are willing to pay for a good over its market price.

Demand curve   A downward-sloping relationship between quantity demanded and price along which income, prices of related goods, tastes, and market size are held constant.

Diminishing marginal productivity   Decreasing extra output as more units of a variable input are combined with fixed inputs.

Diminishing marginal utility   Decreasing extra satisfaction from each additional unit of a good or service consumed.

Discount rate   The extra fraction, D, required to make someone indifferent between having \$1 now and having \$$[1 + D]$ a year from now.

Discrimination   Treating objectively identical people differently.

Diseconomies of scale   Long-run average costs that increase as a firm increases output.

Dominant strategy   A strategy that is best no matter what the other party does.

Economic profit   Revenue minus input costs (including opportunity cost).

Economic rent   The excess of the returns to an input above its opportunity cost.

Economies of scale   Long-run average cost that decreases as a firm increases output.

Efficiency   Using all resources and producing all goods in a way that minimizes cost and maximizes consumer surplus.

Elastic demand   Quantity demanded decreasing by more than 1 percent with each 1 percent rise in price.

Equilibrium price   The price that equates the demand and the supply for a good or service.

Equity   Fairness.

Externality   A cost or benefit conferred on others by the maximizing behavior of a person, firm, or government.

Fixed cost   Input cost that does not vary in the short run because it has already been incurred.

Free rider   Someone who benefits from a public good without paying for it.

Globalization   The expansion of trade and production across international borders.

Human capital   Skills and knowledge embodied in workers as a result of previous investments of time and goods.

Import quotas   Numerical limits on the amounts of particular goods allowed to be imported.

Income elasticity of demand   The percentage change in quantity purchased in response to a 1 percent increase in income.

Independence of irrelevant alternatives   The choice between a pair of alternatives is not altered by an offer of a third alternative that is inferior to one or both of the pair.

Inelastic demand   Quantity demanded decreasing by less than 1 percent with each 1 percent rise in price.

Inferior good   A good with a negative income elasticity of demand.

Long-run average cost   The minimum average cost of producing at a particular level of output if the firm plans to produce that amount forever.

Luxury   A good with an income elasticity of demand greater than 1.

Marginal cost   The change in total cost that occurs when output increases by one unit.

Marginal product   The change in total product that occurs when an input is increased by one unit.

Marginal revenue   The change in revenue that occurs when quantity sold increases by one unit.

Marginal revenue product   The change in revenue that occurs when an input is increased by one unit.

Marginal tax rate   The change in taxes when the amount taxed increases by one unit.

Marginal utility   The change in utility from a good when the amount consumed of that good increases by one unit.

Market demand curve   The sum at each price of the demand curves of all the individuals in the market.

Matching   Bringing together buyers and sellers so that they enter into a trade.

Minimum wage   A price floor on a wage rate.

Monopolist   The single seller of a good.

Monopolistic competition   A market characterized by many sellers of similar but not identical goods.

Monopoly   A market with only one seller.

Monopsony   A market with only one buyer.

Nash equilibrium   A strategic situation in which no side in a game has any incentive to alter its strategy.

Necessity   A good with an income elasticity of demand less than 1 but greater than zero.

Negative externality   A cost imposed on others by the maximizing behavior of a person, firm, or government.

Oligopolist   One of a small number of sellers in a market.

Oligopoly   A market characterized by few sellers.

Opportunity cost   The value of an input, good, or service in its best alternative use.

Pareto-improving   A change that improves the well-being of at least one person without reducing anyone else's well-being.

Pareto-optimal   Not being able to improve the well-being of one person without reducing at least one other's well-being.

Positive externality   A benefit conferred on others by the maximizing behavior of a person, firm, or government.

Positive-sum game   A game in which the sum of the payoffs to the players is positive.

Present value   The discounted value of a stream of future income or returns.

Price ceiling   An upper limit imposed on a market price.

Price discrimination   Charging different prices to buyers of a good or service.

Price elasticity of demand   The percentage change in quantity demanded when price rises by 1 percent.

Prisoners' dilemma   A game in which both sides have incentives that lead them to an equilibrium inferior to a collusive equilibrium.

Product differentiation   Creating characteristics of products to distinguish them from other products and make their demand less elastic.

Production possibility frontier   A curve indicating a trade-off between two goods and showing the maximum combinations of them that can be produced with the available resources.

Profit-maximizing   Seeking the highest available difference between revenue and cost.

Progressive tax   A tax with an average tax rate that rises with the amount taxed.

Property rights   Control over a good, service, or set of rules.

Public good   A good whose consumption by one person does not reduce the amount available to be consumed by other people.

Regressive tax   A tax with an average tax rate that falls with the amount taxed.

Revenue   Quantity times price.

Risk-averse   Preferring a choice with a higher chance of an average return to one with higher chances of large gains or large losses.

Shortage   An excess of demand over supply at the current price.

Short-run average total cost   The sum of fixed cost and variable cost divided by the quantity produced.

Speculation   Buying a product at one point in time, hopefully cheaply, and selling it at a later date, hopefully at a higher price.

Subgame perfect   A strategy in a dynamic game that yields the player the best outcome in all future periods.

Subsidy   An amount paid, typically by the government, to reduce the price consumers or firms must pay for a good, service, or productive input.

Substitutes A pair of goods related so that when the price of one falls, the amount of the other that is sold falls.

Superior good A good with a positive income elasticity of demand.

Superstars People whose talents generate immense earnings.

Supply curve An upward-sloping relationship between quantity supplied and price along which technology and input costs are held constant.

Surplus An excess of supply over demand at the current price.

Tariff A tax on an imported good or service.

Tax incidence The share of a tax borne by each side in the market for the taxed good or service.

Tied sale Requiring that a product supplied competitively be purchased together with a monopolized product.

Total cost The sum of fixed cost and variable cost.

Trade-off A choice between two goods or services that, because of scarcity, requires forgoing some of one to obtain more of the other.

Transaction costs Costs of changing the ownership of property rights.

Unit-elastic demand Quantity demanded decreasing by 1 percent with each 1 percent rise in price.

Utility Satisfaction.

Variable cost Input cost that changes as output changes.

Zero-sum game A game in which one side's gain must equal the other side's loss.

Index